The Sociology of Music

The Sociology of Music

Fabio Dasilva, Anthony Blasi,
David Dees

UNIVERSITY OF NOTRE DAME PRESS
Notre Dame, Indiana 46556

Library of Congress Cataloging in Publication Data

Blasi, Anthony J.
   The sociology of music.

   Bibliography: p.
   Includes index.
   1. Music and society. 2. Music—Philosophy and
aesthetics. I. Dasilva, Fabio B. II. Dees, David R.
III. Title.
ML3800.B58   1984   780'.07   83-40597
ISBN 0-268-01710-7

Manufactured in the United States of America

6-3-87

Contents

Preface

Music appeals to people everywhere and has been at the heart of all human societies. The relation, accordingly, between music and society must be considered as fundamental in the world of human beings, and therefore an analysis of music from the perspective of sociology is of immediate interest.

Sociology begins with the fact that people influence one another. What they do and how they do it changes with place and time. Music too represents an instance of people influencing one another in a variety of ways. To understand music as a social process, it is necessary to define and describe it in terms of the basic types of social influence that it brings about in the life of human beings.

For purposes of clarity, it should be understood that the sociology of music is thus not so much about music in itself as about society. Music is one of the forms in which societies become evident to their members. Social reality is embodied in individuals' activities, musical and otherwise. In the same way that we understand something about a person by the way that person speaks to us, dresses, walks, and works, we understand something social about a group or society by the way that music is lived, by the way it supports and influences lives within that society.

In the first chapter music is introduced as a type of mentality and is described as assuming certain unique features. These features then are investigated in subsequent chapters in order to determine how people take part in music conduct, how music conduct is organized, and how certain instances of music phenomena can be understood. The last chapter presents illustrations of how sociologists come to an understanding of particular instances of musical phenomena through the use of their sociological framework. In this part of the work David Dees looks at costuming as an obvious way that many people who engage in musical performance communicate with their audiences. He then uncovers the far less obvious social influences involved in the evolution of the banjo and the way it is played. Next, Anthony Blasi interprets Scott Joplin's opera in the light of American race relations. Finally, Fabio Dasilva looks at one of the piano works of Villa-Lobos to see how it is shaped by the world structure as well as by the homeland society of the composer.

Some of the materials included in this presentation have been made public before in a different form. The critical reaction that they then received as well as the comments raised to other parts of this work by many colleagues have been of great value for the re-elaboration of the material by the authors. We would like in this regard to single out for special thanks: Jeffrey Crane, Jim Faught, and Hernan Vera Godoy. Additional thanks must go to our students at the Universities of Florida, Louisville, and Notre Dame who through their sensitive inquiry helped to shape this work. We also give thanks to Mary Jay for typing, and we are most grateful to Ann Rice for her superb editorial assistance at the Notre Dame Press. Certainly none of them deserve blame for any remaining errors or distortions.

1
Music as Mentality

I. MUSIC IS SOCIAL

It is customary for systematic discussions to begin with a formal definition of the subject under consideration. A treatise in geology, for example, might begin that way, leading the reader to distinguish between geological and nongeological facts. Were we to follow that custom, this inquiry should begin by defining music and perhaps sociology. Unfortunately, our subject matter does not obey the custom. Music does not stand outside of consciousness so as to allow for an objective definition of it in that way; rather music is located inside the very consciousness which would do the defining. Thus our point of departure cannot be a definition; it cannot be a declaration that we know objectively from the beginning what music is and that the reader will be let in on the secret; rather, we have to admit that we cannot readily define music. We must ask for the reader's patience while we explore the difficulties and opportunities of music's definitional problems.

The sociologist has little to contribute to music as music. For purposes of clarity, it should be understood that the sociology of music is not about music but about society. Music is one of the forms in which societies become evident to their members. Social reality is embodied in individuals' activities, musical and otherwise; and these activities constitute social reality. In the same way that we understand something about a person from the way the person speaks to us, dresses, walks, and works, we understand something about that person from the way the person acts musically.

Please notice that we want to look into music, not at it, as one would look into windows and mirrors, not at them. The eyes are focused to a distance beyond the surface of the pane of glass in order to look at something other than the glass. We understand windows and mirrors in a useful way when we look into them rather than at them. So too, we understand music in a useful way when we look into it to see a reality stretching out into an expanse behind it or to see a reflection of ourselves. The reality we wish to

1

see and the aspect of ourselves we wish to comprehend is, in the present case, social. Seeing music as social may not be the most artistic or elegant approach, but it may yet be useful.

The sociology of music can be worthwhile in a way that is analogous to the usefulness of science in general. The history of science reveals that as scientific knowledge has advanced less and less of the world has been left under the sway of superstition. Taking a cue from this history, sociologists try to combat social superstitions. For instance, in the United States they are more or less succeeding in combating racist beliefs, though they are making less headway in combating class bias. Thus "enlightened" people of the age may not be racists today, but they may believe that it is all right to discriminate (e.g., through pricing mechanisms) against the poor. The sociologist assumes that if people understand inequality, they will improve class relations in the way that they have been hoping to improve race relations. Most importantly, people have to be led to see how class assumptions influence their own thoughts, emotions, and actions. The mission of the sociologist is to enhance self-knowledge in this manner. Similarly, the sociology of music is aimed at self-knowledge. It is the hope that people who engage in musical conduct[1] can overcome whatever lack of understanding and whatever social superstitions they have about that activity. In particular the aura of mystery surrounding music needs to be accounted for.

Social Health

On the other hand, if we look at the history of science more closely, we see that it is largely a succession of theories and principles, with the later ones being presumably better in some respect than the earlier ones. The history of music and the other arts is not like that but rather consists of a series of biographies. This is no accident; science accumulates statements about things which exist outside of persons while music and the other arts do not. If one were to study a human phenomenon such as music "scientifically," i.e. by accumulating statements about it as an extramusical reality, a serious error would result. Making a statement about an object is appropriate when the matter at hand is really an object, but music is not an object. Music does not exist independently of subjectivity. To speak of it as if it did would therefore misrepresent it. Thus a genuinely scientific approach, i.e., a truly knowledgeable approach, must operate on different principles than those of the natural sciences. Sociology often finds itself having to use principles which emanate out of the subjective nature of humanity; hence, the fact that music is only found in biographies poses no insurmountable difficulty for it. Society itself only exists in biographies of individuals.[2]

It is precisely the subjective nature of music which makes it impossible for us to define it. Definitions are statements which draw boundaries around objects, separating them from other objects. If music is not objective, it cannot be defined in this traditional way. It can, however, be discussed intelligently, provided that the intelligence in question does not attempt to make it into an object. The appropriate description will have to be structured around the contours of knowledge itself, the countours of the tension between subject and object, the contours of the very mode in which music comes to the subject's awareness.

The question which must first be asked, then, is not, What is music? but: How shall we approach music? Our answer is that we shall approach music as a mentality. A mentality is a mode of mental conduct which characterizes some social collectivity that holds it in common. Mental conduct is a kind of activity in which individual humans engage, but a mentality is shared by a number of humans. Our approach takes music to be mentalistic, as opposed to mental. It is in this sense that we said above that the sociology of music is about society rather than about music; it focuses on the mentalities which musical conduct embodies. More precisely, it focuses on the way people are related to one another's activity in music; it focuses on sociability as evidenced in music (Silbermann, 1963: 6-8, 37).

The suggestion is that musical conduct is inter-human, interpersonal, or social (Mueller, 1963: 216). While musical conduct may at times be private, it is still social in the same way that thought is social. Just as people think in languages, which are very social constructs of shared grammars and symbols, so also they create, interpret, make or hear music, which is a social construct. Moreover, they use their imaginations to present music to themselves, which is to say that they imagine a social situation in which a presentation, interchange, or performance imaginatively takes place as if two parties were oriented to one another. A musician practicing in solitude, for example, must take on the attitude of a second party in order to assess the practice performance. In effect, one asks how a critic, teacher, or authority would assess the practice performance. As a composer writing in solitude, one must view one's own work as a tentative product, from the perspective of an imaginary other, to decide if what is about to be written is indeed what is desired. The process has parallels with playing chess

with oneself, where actions are assessed in terms of future consequences. It is the genius of humans that they are social even when
they are alone.

All the arts are social in this sense. But music is social in
another way as well: it involves a committee of composer, interpreter, and listener. It is a performing art. The performing is
social in a way that athletic performances, for example, are not;
for an athlete can sometimes perform (e.g., in running a mile)
without enacting someone else's thoughts. A musician enacts a
second person's intentions, the composer's; and a composer's
creation does not reach fulfillment until performed, at which time
it succeeds or fails in taking on a life of its own. Similarly a performance is but a practice until heard. Thus, the sociology of music
has an inherent problematic that the sociology of some other arts
do not have — that of the social existence of the musical deed
(Supicic, 1964:121).

To describe music as social is to assume that actors influence
one another. The specific media through which the influence is
transmitted varies — different instruments in live performance;
score notations within a recognized genre of composition; radio;
phonograph; interactive interpretation through re-creation in
ensemble, etc. The influence itself takes the social form of different
persons' experiential biographies going through parallel or reciprocal sequences. There is a "flux of tones unrolling in inner time"
(Shutz, 1951: 88).[3] The stream of consciousness of each participant runs through an interplay of recollections, retentions,
protentions, and anticipations. In this way individuals who may be
far removed from one another by history and geography experience
a parallel or reciprocal subjective state; they have something in
common. The suggestion is not that they have identical experiences.
Experiences are necessarily grounded in individual nervous systems
and hence cannot be shared; there is no guarantee that one person's
toothache is felt in precisely the same way as another person's.
Rather, the suggestion is that there is relatedness between two or
more subjectivities. The streams of consciousness involved travel
through similar (but probably not identical) material. They have a
mentality in common, even if their unique mental orientations to
that mentality are not held in common.

One of the interesting consequences of this fellow-traveling
through musical material is that the patterns of rights and obligations institutionalized in a society remain the same across different
musical media. In the United States, a society considerably institu-

tionalized through property rights and contract relationships, similar forms of guaranteeing these rights have developed around different aspects of the world of musical activity. Record companies and radio stations directly or indirectly pay composers' and performers' collectives when they market those persons' music. The record companies pay a royalty to the American Federation of Musicians, and the radio stations pay one to either the American Society of Composers and Publishers or to Broadcast Music, Incorporated.[4] The social relationship established through the unrolling of tones in inner time entails reciprocal rights and duties which have become institutionalized in a very pragmatic way. The business consequences of the social relationship of which we speak illustrate how real it is.

There is another inherent aspect of sociality which is readily evidenced in musical conduct — community. Communities are the limited circles in which particular relationships take place. One's social world does not extend indefinitely but rather reaches only as far as one's reputation. Communities may take the form of a physical settlement, as in the case of villages, neighborhoods, and small towns, or they may be coterminous with small occupation or interest groups, or even factions and organizations. One of the marks of musical conduct which illustrates its social aspect is its communal nature. Some musical communities are marked by particular styles, schools, and standards. Others focus on certain business markets. Others still arise as alternatives to market-oriented communities. The Eastman School in Rochester, for instance, has been important to some composers as an alternative to the musical capital of the United States, New York City.[5]

By now the main lines of our later discussions can be anticipated. Music will be described but not defined, described from a point of view which is at one and the same time subjective and collective. Music will thus be approached as a mentality, whose forms establish interconnections among humans, i.e., social processes. These social processes take on secondary aspects of institutionalization within the framework of larger societies (e.g., the business orientation of the United States). One may not have an adequate grasp of music after appreciating this social existence alone, but one will not understand musical conduct as it occurs without such a knowledge. The sociology of music may not add to the artistic dimensions of music, but it provides a window and mirror to much that is human in music just the same. Its promise is thus both modest and pretentious, much like sociology itself.

II. DIALECTIC OF THE INTENDED AND UNINTENDED

When someone approaches music as a mentality, he or she encounters an immediate paradox. Individuals with their own unique mental processes engage in musical conduct, but music, as a form of social expression, transcends the individual. While the intentions which result in music are individual, music itself is collective. While the personal histories which lead up to musical creation, performance, and appreciation are many, the musical traditions which are brought into play at any one time are few. The social unity and individual pluralism seem to need each other in music. Thus music is both singular and plural, social and individual, public and personal. When reduced to simple propositional logic, this is all contradictory; any resolution would require some complex reasoning. When viewed dialectically, it is not a difficult matter at all.

As used in the present discussion, *dialectics* refers to emergent totalities which need to be recognized before individual elements can be assessed.[6] Dialectical phenomena commonly occur in everyday life, where consciousness is a factor in the constitution of relevant processes. Consider two people washing a car; the actions of either one of them can only be insufficiently understood when taken in isolation from the entire project. Indeed, the actions are somewhat meaningless taken out of the context of the social significance of clean or dirty cars. One person may at any one moment think only of wringing a sponge, but there is an important aspect of the situation which transcends that thought, and the significance of having a clean car may not have been thought out by either of the persons at all. A mentality of neatness or cleanliness or presentability may be most fundamental but most out of mind.

Similarly a conversation has more to it than any one person means to say at any one moment in it. Conversations are not speeches, where actors decide ahead of time what words and gestures will be used. Conversations take shape in time, while they are occurring; they are enacted in the same moment that actors decide what to say. The course of the conversation emerges, with one statement depending on the others. The next statement is elicited by the present one in such a way that it will be related to it, but there is a certain openness wherein one cannot predict accurately just what the next statement will be. Moreover, the total significance of a conversation is more than what is said in the individual sentences; the very fact that the conversation took place may be far more important than what was said. After a misunderstanding, for example, one party can plead that he had talked something over with another party, implying thereby that he had been open and not deceitful about the issue in question prior to the misunderstanding developing. Similarly, the various congressional and judicial proceedings concerning the "Watergate" scandal were focused as much on who conversed with whom at what time as on what was said, because the very occurrence of a conversation implied that people could have asked questions which should have been asked. The "could" and "should" emanate from the possibilities inherent in a conversation rather than what any one actor meant to say.

Dialectical thought thus takes it for granted that the whole is greater or other than the sum of its parts, that meaningful assessments emanate from something other than individual intentions, that important realities cannot be foreseen or predicted, that actors may not know the full significance of their deeds, and that intentions are relevant to more than what they intend. Dialectical thought offers a method of thinking about paradox, tragedy, and surprise, where there is a disjuncture between intention and consequence.

As we have said, music is subjective; it is not existent in the social world as an object. This attribute of music is relevant to the dialectical nature of music because subjective realities can entail disjunctures between individual meaning and external consequence more readily than objective realities. Objective realities confront humans as brute facts, and subjective or peculiar responses to such brute facts may be thought of as transitory and rather beside the point. In contrast, in subjective reality the person contributes to the very existence of the reality; its outcome may be as shocking as brute facts can be, but it would not occur on its own.

While all that is human may well be dialectical, musical conduct is characterized by a greater disjuncture between intention and result than other forms of conscious activity — e.g., language. In the case of language, each symbol calls to mind a universal category or relationship, a general meaning which is comprehended by any number of persons. The universal may even be called to mind by different symbols, as in the case of different languages each having their own words for the same kind of object. Language is constructed around universal or potentially universal ideas which may be correctly or incorrectly applied to objects. Languages may even embody absolute truths which exist only in the realm of pure thought — e.g., the algebraic principle that equals added to equals renders equals. Music does not deal in such universals. Contrary to common belief, there is no universal musical language. While language communicates through allusions to universal ideas on one hand and to objects on the other, music has a different nature. It does not allude but actualizes; it is an executant form of expression (Ortega y Gasset, 1975: 147).

Of course music may serve nonmusical purposes. Some works function as emblems, such as national anthems and theme songs. These indeed refer to things, allude. But music as music does not do this. Even so called program music takes the hearer through a temporal experience full of anticipations and retentions to create an executant effect. While anthems and theme songs are selected arbitrarily and can be changed, the public willing, much in the same way that national flags and state flowers can be changed, program music cannot be arbitrarily substituted without evoking a different experience (see Dufrenne, 1967: 314).

Now let us illustrate what is meant by the dialectical nature of music creating an unintended consequence. Twentieth century American popular music has been interpreted as a case in point. While there are exceptions, in general it has been standardized into a form which is easily recognized: thirty-two bars with a range limited to one octave plus one note. The whole is pre-given and is accepted by the listener, with only the details changing from one hit to another. While serious music has details which acquire sense only in relation to preceding and following developments, popular music's details make sense only in distinguishing one ditty from another. Thus while the harmonic, rhythmic, and melodic structure of some popular music may be more sophisticated than that of some serious music, the standardization and the lack of development from detail to detail keep it from being "serious." "The composition hears for the listener. This is how popular music divests the listener of his spontaneity and promotes conditional reflexes" (Adorno and Simpson, 1941: 22).

Unlike other consumer goods, there is no technological reason for popular music to be standardized. Nonstandardization would not raise the cost of production. This is a good clue for us that some unanticipated consequence of a little-thought-about aspect of the popular music form may be highly relevant to our assessment of it. The standardization is not an accident of technology but a form of imitation. Each song is an attempt to duplicate the success of previous "hits," and variations which distinguish one product from another hide the predigested nature of something designed to be accepted as a mere substitute for something similar. Thus there is a tight normative order, a rigid set of expectations. Even in jazz the order prevails while the improvisations serve as embellishments around it. "Popular music becomes a multiple-choice questionnaire" in the sense that one selects an alternative whose form is already predetermined (Adorno and Simpson, 1941: 22, 26). That the music has a sameness to it from one hit to another is evidenced by the fact that plugging is required to make one product stand out from the others.

The underlying mentality in this kind of music seems to be a responsiveness to a superordinate or authoritarian order. In choosing the embellishments, in expressing preferences for the details, in showing individuality in the particulars, the listener is accepting the foreordained structure. In short, the listener does something unthinkingly which he or she would refuse to do thinkingly — generating enthusiasm for tweedle-dum over tweedle-dee, while being happy to fit into the provided consumer structure. Any greater involvement in the music comes not from a further evolving of tones in inner time but from a heightened subordination to the godlike structure.

> The mania behaviors manifest entrancement in the technical sense of being entirely possessed by the experience. . . . The regularity of rhythm is enhanced by the over-balance of the bass and percussion. The output of excessively high volume creates a physiological sensory response which floods one's sensory modality. Reiteration of thematic and verbal material . . . also creates a hypnotic effect. (Davies, 1969: 279)

Despite the ruckus, it seems to be a psychological equivalent of submission.

Enthusiasts for popular music may well resent the interpretation given above and first formulated by Theodor W. Adorno. If there is any truth to it, that very resentment would manifest the kind of disjuncture between the intended and the unintended which occurs in dialectical relationships. The resentful enthusiast merely approves of the intended aspect and finds little to be happy about in an assessment offered from the perspective of the unintended mentality. The point here is not simply to agree or disagree with the late Theodor Adorno but to see the potential of musically induced mentalities. Through music one may connect himself with the larger social world by means of a similar mentality — e.g., that of the subservience of the multiple-choice questionnaire — made palatable through the disguise of the musical form itself.

Consider again the psychological description quoted above: "The mania behaviors. . . ." This was an account of the musical experience of the rebellious generation of the 1960s. It was a generation at odds with the general societal structure, but no generation is an island; it must ground itself in a continuity with a past and a future. A generation per se simply is not a very reliable entity with which to be identified. The more that generation of the sixties individualized itself in music, the more its embellishments became different from what came before, the more it indirectly satisfied the desire to submit to a stable societal structure. The authoritarian, inflexible rhythm, the hypnotic power of the repetition, the immediate acceptance of the theme, all provided a structure which would have been unacceptable in language. Language would have to have referred to an unacceptable accumulation of objective situations. Was it an accident that in the jazz era, a generation earlier, the music of the former slave sector of the society attained middle-class acceptance and served a similar function? Perhaps the managed society of the fifties stealthily brought management into the leisure hours through jazz, while the lost generation of the sixties found itself, after all, in beatlemania.

III. MEANING IN MUSIC

In the previous section we distinguished between the executant mode of musical expression and the mode of allusion which may be found when music serves some nonmusical purpose — e.g., an emblemic function. Various terminologies have been used to refer to this same distinction. Max Kaplan (1951: 25) distinguished between the *aesthetic function* of music, wherein the performance relates listeners to materials, forms, sounds, or contents inherent within the artistic creation, and the *social function,* wherein it relates its listeners to persons, ideas, cultural norms, or patterns of conduct. His phraseology was misleading because the aesthetic function is as social as are the nonaesthetic functions; the inherent contents of music emanate from the social relationships which are established among composer, performer, and listener.[7] Nevertheless terming the nonaesthetic functions "social" reminds us that there are numerous sociological phenomena which derive from extramusical meanings of music.

Among the more important extramusical meanings are affective meanings (emotions such as happiness, sadness, fear, anger), descriptive meanings (the sea, birds, battles), value meanings (good, bad, ugly, beautiful), and technical meanings, usually couched in the jargon of the music specialist (Wright, 1975: 420). These are nonmusical in the sense that they can be brought to mind as effectively by language or other symbolic forms as by music. Some of them, especially the affective and value meanings, have taken on added importance in the modern phenomenon of canned mood music. The electric phonograph has given nonmusicians power over music so that persons who control physical space are able to determine selection and volume. Similarly the motion picture industry uses sound tracks as "background music" which sets a desired mood. As additional life speaces come to be sound-tracked in this manner, the whole arrangement takes on a manipulative aspect. People arranging various kinds of interaction settings — e.g., preparing parties with different sexual compositions or with different kinds of narcotic stimulants such as alcohol or marijuana — have been shown to use different kinds of music to help set the appropriate mood (Dees and Vera, 1978). It is as if the contemporary host, merchant, and mall manager feel compelled to provide us with a soundtrack to induce us to do what they want us to do. Thus some radio stations direct their programming, not at a kind of listener who will willingly tune them in, but rather provide "airport music" for social manipulators who in turn foist it off on the "trackees" as atmosphere. Music thus has become a major component of canned ambient.[8]

However, such extramusical uses are not the sum and substance of meaning in music. When Leonard Bernstein composed his effective sound track for the motion picture *On the Waterfront,* for instance, he was not simply bringing familiar associations into play in order to produce a mood; the music had nothing particularly familiar about it when it was first heard in the theaters. Similarly, the better opera scores do not use mere formulae, though through overuse, imitation, and sometimes simplified rendition [9] they have been turned into formulae. Rather, the better theater scores evolve in a dynamic of their own wherein the listener is not only called upon to live through the unfolding of the music in his or her own biographical experience, but to do so as though a witness to the social situation which is being portrayed. We will return to the social psychological complex entailed in this genre of music in a later chapter; for the present it is merely important to notice the differences between nonmusical meanings and musical meanings. The nonmusical derives from associations available to the listener through his or her memory of the current culture; a piece of music may have once elicited musical meaning but may have lost it through repetition and association with something else. It is hard, for example, for most of us to hear the wedding music from Mendelssohn's "Incidental Music to *A Midsummer Night's Dream*" as music rather than as a recollection of nuptial ceremony. Theater music may be either mere track music which calls to mind such prepackaged associations, or it may have genuine musical meaning for the hearer.

It has already been pointed out that musical meanings are as social as are nonmusical ones. Anything which occurs as an interaction among persons is social, and music occurs as an interaction among composer, performer, and listener. However, social realities have another dimension to them wherein no interaction occurs in isolation but rather in a larger context. To make a comparison with language: one person cannot say anything to another with any meaningful effect unless there is first a recognized custom of mutual orientation (e.g., conversation) and a language comprised of a grammatical system and vocabulary. Similarly, composers do not throw dots on paper, performers do not emit sounds, and listeners do not merely have their eardrums vibrate; there are systems of music which serve as reference points for musical composition, performance, and listening. In short, musical interaction always occurs in a musical culture.

According to the Gestalt psychologists, perception does not occur in a manner which allows isolated stimuli to register in a central nervous system but rather occurs in organized ensembles of stimuli (see Kohler, 1947). People do not hear sounds but groups of sounds which they recognize as chirps, buzzes, words, and crashes. They do not see spots of light but rather shapes and sizes in three dimensions. Their social existence results in many of the Gestalts or groupings of stimuli being patterned according to principles held in common sometimes by whole civilizations and sometimes by small groups. Music is as subject to this tendential regularity as any other social activity. Thus no composition is created in a vacuum; it imitates, extends, violates, or reacts against some pattern which has preceded it. No performer encounters a score without bringing to it as much as will be found in it. No listener merely responds in the manner of a microphone crystal or a stretch of magnetic tape. However unsatisfactory one's musical preparation may be, no socialized person, nobody who can either grunt intelligibly or be grunted at intelligibly, is musically virgin territory.

The inevitable consequence of this is that music never repeats itself, despite the efforts of the popular music industry. We do not hear Mozart's music as his audiences heard it because we hear it from the perspective of people who have heard post-Mozartian music. However much we may attempt to appreciate the intent of Mozart himself, there remains an inherent perspectival difference. Even when the exact sounds which rattled the composer's ear-drums rattle ours — say, those generated by the famous recording of Mascagni conducting his *Cavalleria Rusticana* — we will have a slightly different Gestalt from the original. Moreover, we cannot hear the same work twice and hear it in the same way both times. Thus when we speak of a musical culture, we are not referring to some static state of affairs which is thinglike but rather something as tentative, as engaged, as charcterized by a to-and-fro activity as a ping-pong game. Cultures do not exist; they are made, remade, and unmade.

It is this peculiarity of musical meaning which gives rise to the unique nature of musical competence.[10] Those who have a mastery of one or more music technologies may be said to be more competent in music than those who have no such mastery. Since people in many settings tend to be sensitive about their competencies, this factor alone gives rise to interesting activities: making invidious comparisons, creating authoritative arbitrations, establishing stratification (i.e., ranking) systems, faking, etc. This occurs in any cultural sector where there is unequal access to or mastery of a valued gnosis. But with music the relatively unlettered do not exist in cultural isolation; indeed the technical experts may experience the isolative aspects of the situation. Between total incompetence and total mastery — two fairly rare kinds of cases — is the portion of the spectrum taken up by the music follower whose competence is "an implicit mastery and mere internalization of interpretation schemes" (Wright, 1975: 426). The knowledge of interpretation schemes enables the listener to anticipate what is to be heard and to connect it with what has gone before. To avoid boredom, the anticipations need to be open, much like a question; they need to point to a territory defined by certain horizons, but not predict precisely where in that territory the next phenomenon is to be found (see Gadamer, 1975: 325ff.). The logical structure of the question allows for a certain randomness in the answer, provided the questioner is prepared for such discourse. In small talk, for instance, relative randomness is in order, while in legal proceedings getting off a topic may give rise to objections. Similarly, in aleatory music chance is anticipated as a factor in the interpretive scheme. When musical understanding has failed to occur, what has happened is that the interpretive scheme has escaped the listener (or performer).

The material of interpretive schemes includes harmony, rhythm, and melody. Each of these represents a subsystem of sounds codified by a long and prestigious tradition, which must be known ahead of time. In the case of harmony, it is within a sounding space that each sound becomes a note, that is, an element of the totality. Apart from a scale, a single sound has no meaning. Moreover, the chosen scale or key exerts a certain power of attraction or repulsion vis-à-vis other sounds. While a given musical genre may set some of the rules which serve as the relevant meaning-providing context to a sound, each individual composition comprises an ad hoc system of rules as well (Dasilva and Dees, 1975: 8). Even in avoiding certain harmonic conventions, a composer must follow rigorous counter rules of his or her own making. (In social anthropology, avoidance rules are an important aspect of social organization.) In any case, the listener's perception itself implies a dynamic once a system has been established and a given sound is placed into a relationship with it.

Rhythm renders sensible a stream of sound through its decomposition into beats which proportion duration and vary accents. The rhythmic structure itself may be a simple identifiable type or constitute a unique polyrhythmic pattern which must be grasped as a whole. It is not necessary that rhythmic schemes be clearly identified, as in an academic analysis, for it is enough that they are felt and produce an internal movement which places us on the same plane as the composition. The rhythmic scheme is something of the composition and not a mere measure imposed on it from outside (Dasilva and Dees, 1975: 14). However much a composer may wish to be free of rhythmic constraints, it is nevertheless inevitable that the composition must exist in time. Traditional rhythmic schemes may be set aside as traditional harmonic schemes may be, but music cannot exist outside of time and space. Hence even the most innovative work will entail the establishment of interpretive schemes — albeit ad hoc ones.

Melody differs from harmony and rhythm insofar as it is its own measure. It is not a scheme used to interpret something else but is itself a specific Gestalt. While harmony and rhythm are fields, dimensions, melody is an identification, a meaning. This does not prevent a composition from having multiple melodies because the unity of a work of that kind supports several identifiable elements (Dasilva and Dees, 1975: 19). Even when randomness is introduced as a thematic device, it sets identifying horizons for a work's progression.

In summary, musical meaning occurs in musical culture. While the term *musical culture* may refer equally well to the conventions of conduct in concerts and other musical settings, as used in the present context it refers to the recognition of rules, recipes, and interpretation schemes of music itself (Wright, 1975: 428). It pertains in this narrow sense to music per se rather than to allusions which musical works may take on.

IV. SOCIAL RELATIVITY

In various scientific circles in the nineteenth century, it was thought that the social world was predetermined by the physical world. "National character," whatever that was, was explained by the climate, diet, and terrain to which the nation in question was exposed. Genetic inheritance was thought to explain intelligence. Evolution was interpreted to say that whoever held power, property, and prestige deserved it because they were more fit (see Hofstadter, 1955). Anthropologists and sociologists began to attack such notions when they discovered the importance of culture in structuring different social collectivities; such ideas were shown by them to be social superstitions, to be mere class, race, and national prejudices in scientific disguise. They found that the social world was organized around meanings and that they had to learn a people's meaning system or culture before they could understand anything about that people's lifeways. "Cultural relativity" came to be seen as a necessity in social science; the scientist could not assume his or her own meaning system was superior or that other cultures could be appreciated adequately by merely ranking them in the order that they approximated one's own culture. Since cultures and meanings are mentalistic, dynamic, and dialectical, something fixed like the physical realm which could be described with unchanging principles did not seem to be a likely place to find new explanations for the cultural universe. Today physical explanations of cultural phenomena sound as strange to the sociologist's ears as the suggestion that Finland's northerly location explains the music of Sibelius' sounds in the ears of a musicologist.

In the study of music the idea of relativity has some necessary implications. One must accept the idea that different collectivities of people order and assess their music by quite different principles and that therefore one cannot say that one collectivity's music is better or worse than another's. The claim that there are absolute, universal standards in the arts suddenly becomes a fiction of romantic philosophy (Mueller, 1935). Extravagant claims to "taste" become admissions of one's narrow focus on one culture — and probably only one facet of a culture at that. This can be quite unnerving for people who take too seriously the status-hierarchy which may have developed in any one musical world. The virtuoso soloist and the rock star find themselves somehow similar to the remote tribal chanter and, worst of all, similar to one another.

In order to set music apart from other cultural phenomena and to make it an equal to science, musical commentators have sought fixed principles with which to dignify music. Music was to become a thing which could be defined by harmony, rhythm, and melody. Thus a natural science of sound was to stand somewhere in an inner essence of music. This, of course, established a contradiction between how people conceived of music on the one hand and how they actually experienced music on the other. "For precisely in its endeavor to defend its integrity, music produces from within itself traits of that very nature against which it struggles" (Adorno, 1973: xv). The executant experience of the unfolding of forms is simply inconsistent with abstract, static concepts. Theodor W. Adorno used this inconsistency as a point of departure for his critique of twentieth century musical movements. While abstract categories are more accessible to thought about music than is the music itself, while they therefore aid thinking, he considered it erroneous to force music to conform to them:

> Truth or untruth . . . cannot be determined by a mere discussion of categories, such as atonality, twelve-tone technique, or neo-classicism; but only in the concrete crystalization of such categories in the structure of music itself. (Adorno, 1973: 4-5)

He objected to Igor Stravinsky's attempt to bring contemporary music back to an idea of what music once was, and he even had reservations about Arnold Schoenberg's implicit assumption that departures from such a traditional idea constituted progress. In both cases, the composers were setting out from abstract categories rather than from musical experience itself.

Whether or not one agrees with Adorno with respect to Stravinsky's neoclassical compositions and Schoenberg's compositional intentions, Adorno's basic insight is an instrutive one: musical progress occurs in music and not in ideas about music. He belonged to the Frankfurt School of social philosophy, which was generally critical of the intellectualistic tendencies of modern social thought. Modern social thought has modeled itself after the natural sciences, treating "society" as a thing or object. Those who engage in such thinking blind themselves to the most important thing about social reality — they themselves make it. Our subjectivity and our society's objectivity are inextricably intertwined, and as soon as we depict social reality as an object external to ourselves we falsify our knowledge of it. We carry around in our memories an incorrect idea of an object rather than attune ourselves to the social processes in which we are taken up. The Frankfurt School, using certain Marxian insights, saw that this kind of incorrect thinking fit well into social patterns which were unfair; the beneficiaries of an unjust world would not see how they helped maintain injustice and hence would not feel guilty; the victims would see their plight as part of the natural, objectlike order of things and hence would not feel victimized. In sociological terminology, an intellectualistic approach to social reality which made social constructions seem natural and objective rather than contrived and subjective was an "ideology."

In Adorno's mind, the Frankfurt School's social critique of this kind of ideology provided a basis for a critique of music. An objectivist approach to music, an approach which falsified music itself so that it would be experienced as an instance of some preexisting idea of music rather than experienced in terms of the experience itself, would be a cultural training ground for an unjust world's culture. If a person can be led to intellectualize music, if he or she could make even music thinglike in the midst of a flow of experience, then objectifying anything else in the social world, making the most contrived and unnatural arrangements seem natural, would be a cinch. Note that the underlying Adornian critique is the same whether applied to the industry products of either serious or popular music, which he saw as mere thinglike commodities. In both cases, the individual is led through a cultural boot camp in which a numbness appropriate for an absurd future is acquired devotedly.

The relative nature of music not only leads us to reject the idea that there are fixed musical standards and to be suspicious of developments based on ideas of music as opposed to music itself, but it also leads to an appreciation of the historical dynamic of music. "Because the musical experience develops in time, it is not legitimate to seek it in an enjoyment which has been experienced before" (Silbermann, 1963: 75).[11] Since the meaning of a composition changes with the passage of time, since it is not heard at a later point in time in the same way as when it was first performed, it is also true that styles characteristic of a large number of works also change in meaning. Someone hoping to write in a new style in 1800 will depart from a different body of music than someone entertaining the same hope in 1900. Music involves spontaneity, originality, freshness, and similar intents which have inherent dynamics; even the intent of being faithful to tradition entails an inherent changeableness, since the catalog of untraditional contaminants would have to be revised unceasingly.[12] Moreover, the intent itself is a change since what is now a classic was not such when first performed; the original had no preservative intent. To put it crudely, the classics did not always sound classical.

Not only does the meaning of any one work change, but trends in the performances change as well. Evidence of this is hard to obtain since "actual musical performances are, of course, ephemeral and can only be recaptured by means of historical documents. In this respect they differ from architecture, literature, and other forms of material human achievement" (Mueller, 1951: 4). However, it is commonly known that performance pitch in general has changed, that the focus has shifted away from soloists' demonstrations of pyrotechnics and toward the revelation of musical material, that composers' intended tempos seem unrealistically fast or slow as time passes, etc.[13] The fact that performances are more frequent than in past centuries, with the rise of more orchestras with full seasons, and the fact that performances are more available because of recordings and radio, suggests that both performance styles and composition styles will come and go more rapidly than in the past. While conductors will at best have liberty, but not license, for many years to come, the day is past when a Beethoven can dominate repertory for a hundred and fifty years (Mueller, 1951: 391).

We are dealing here with fashion. Change would be a source of chaos and incomprehensibility if the social world were organized around fixed principles and meanings. "Fashion introduces a conspicuous measure of unanimity and uniformity in what would otherwise be a markedly fragmented arrangement" (Blumer, 1969: 289). It achieves in a dynamic society what custom accomplishes in a settled society. While in common parlance fashion may imply a superficial conformity to the latest trends, in the present context it simply means that cultural changes occur collectively and inevitably rather than individually and accidentally. To understand music as a social phenomenon requires a sensitivity to the fashion of musical conduct, to the changing expectations which contribute to the structuring of that conduct.

The history of modern Western art music has witnessed a continual tension between conservative and progressive forces. The established conventions have been increasingly violated amidst considerable upheaval in the musical community (Rieger, 1978: 3). The three great pillars of western music: harmony, rhythm, melody, which had been accorded an almost dogmatic standing at the beginning of the contemporary period, have been subjected to a dramatic series of challenges. The harmonic practices featured by Beethoven had been stretched to the limit in the work of Wagner, Mahler, and Richard Strauss. After the adventurism of Debussy, what was left was annihilated by Schoenberg in the 1920s. With Debussy, there was no conventional melodic line but rather, short melodic fragments floating in a wash of orchestral color. In 1913 Stravinsky's *Rite of Spring* caused a celebrated riot with its highly percussive, irregular rhythms and absence of any recognizable melodic element. While Stravinsky changed course from this and went in another direction, he set a precedent for George Antheil, Edgar Varese, and others.

> [Stravinsky] was villified as a "destroyer," rather than a creator, of music. Antheil gained a reputation as the "bad boy" of music, while Varese became identified as something of a madman. The musical clientele of the period reacted as if it has been grossly insulted by such composers. (Rieger, 1978: 5-6)

As noted before, the subsequent developments took a rationalistic turn, which even gave pause to a sophisticated thinker like Adorno, who thought Schoenberg had led music out of its executant mode by intellectualizing it. The new approach seemed to be an imitation of the natural sciences, complete with experiments. John Gage's music has no traces of tradition, and the works of Milton Babbitt and Yannis Xenakis have introduced the complete and precise mathematical determination of all sounds (Malhotra, 1979).

There is no inherent reason why the traditional selection, organization, and repetition patterns of sounds (see Rieger, 1978) should be considered normal music and the "revolutionary" ones unnatural. The feeling of naturalness is entirely a matter of social construction. What one generation sets up as an arrangement of convenience the next receives as a fixed order of the universe (see Berger and Luckmann, 1967). Music plays upon this sense of naturalness, seeming innovative when it launches out from the conventional but not outrageous when it somehow seems to be grounded in it. With increasing familiarity, the spectrum of possibilities that seems natural becomes progressively extended. The recent history of Western art music has seen such a wide expansion of accepted musical grammars that the principle of relativity has to be applied within a culture as much as across cultures. The "man in the street" may find the music of his next door neighbor as unfamiliar as the incidental chant of an Inca victory celebration. Social relativity thus may be seen as a dynamic principle of musical history, with different persons inhabiting different centuries. For no one person will history stand completely still because perhaps the only universal in music — relativity — impels it to stay at least a few steps ahead of cliché.

V. MULTIPLE REALITIES AND MUSIC

Sociologists have found a philosophical tradition called phenomenology to be very useful as a model of the social world. Phenomenology began as a method of thought in which a person studied the structure of knowledge; it was thought turning back upon itself. One could focus on the differences between awareness, experience, reasoning, and other musical phenomena. The point of departure for these considerations was that we do not have direct access to the realities outside of our own subjectivity but only the appearances (phenomena) of those realities. Indeed even our subjectivities themselves are available for our inspection only through appearances. In order to study the way we create these appearances for ourselves and the various kinds of them which we create, phenomenology leads the individual thinker through mental experiments which set aside the contents or meanings of experiences and thoughts in order to look at the experiences and thoughts themselves.

The early phenomenological essays of Edmund Husserl were formulated in an attempt to reveal the limits of natural science (Husserl, 1962, 1970). The natural sciences made statements about realities whose existence is independent of our awareness of them. There is an assumption in such science that the physical world respects logical relationships; as one plus one logically yields two, one quart mixed with another quart should yield two quarts. While in the physical world this is not always a valid assumption (e.g., one quart of water mixed with one quart of alcohol yields less than two quarts), it is in the social world that the assumption is most often invalid. In logic, if A is greater than B and B is greater than C, then A is greater than C; in the social world if A has power over B and B has power over C, it does not follow that A has power over C rather than vice-versa. In the social world much depends on the subjective and intersubjective construction of each relationship. There is an ad hoc and individual dimension which results in a disjuncture between the logical and the enacted. While logic exists in eternity, sociality exists in time; society is historical.

Since, to use the language of a previous section, social realities are mentalistic, and since music is one of these mentalistic realities, a philosophical approach which helps us understand and describe mental (individual) and mentalistic (shared) phenomena may provide us with some useful insights. We will not be emphasizing the criticism of the natural science approach here, which was one of Husserl's main concerns, nor will we focus on epistemological questions in general. Rather we will look for the structure of mentality as described by phenomenology wherever that structure is made evident in musical conduct. That is to say, a particular description of awareness and mentality will be taken as a description of music. In the same way that the physicist assumes there is a correspondence between mathematical relationships and physical ones, we will assume that there is a correspondence between some of our thoughts about mentality on the one hand and musically enacted mentality on the other.

The Awareness Tension

Let us begin with the activity which we call awareness. Musical awareness is simply an instance of awareness in general. In awareness there is a subject, a person, who is oriented toward some object, a thing. This orientation is a subject-object relationship, a tension which is relaxed only with the cessation of the awareness. In the hope of describing awareness itself, we want to focus on the activities, materials, and states which comprise that tension. We are not interested in either the subject or the object but in the tension. So we will put the subject and the object out of mind and not concern ourselves with them. We will simply suspend any beliefs we may have about them. This logical procedure of suspending any concern with an aspect of awareness (in this case, the subject and the object) is called the *epoche*. In meditating upon the subject-object tension, we ignore subject and object, we enter into a double epoche, in order to address the tension itself.

If there is a correspondence between our thoughts about mentality (e.g., epoches) on the one hand and musically enacted mentality on the other, then we should find enacted epoches in musical conduct. We should find, for instance, that music suspends any concern with either objects or with subjectivity. Focusing either on things or on oneself during musical conduct would be experienced as a distraction because it would take one away from the awareness tension itself where musical meaning occurs. Music is made of states, acts, and materials, in this case, which make up such a tension; it thus comprises a mentality wherein an awareness focuses only on these states, acts, and materials.

In philosophical phenomenology several distinctions are made between different aspects of the awareness tension. Beginning with the aspect which is closest to the object side of the subject-object tension, there are material constructs. These are realities, such as color, feeling, and tone, which do not exist in the natural world but rather exist in our experiences as a result of the impact of the natural world on us. Color, for instance, is a construct of the effect of light waves of various frequencies on the nervous system associated with the eyes. When the nervous system is not sufficiently activated, as in the case of dim light, there is not more color, irrespective of the frequencies of the faint light waves. This realm of material constructs is obviously important in music. The involvement is not with the objects which produce sounds (e.g., piano strings) but the sounds as heard. Equally obvious is the fact that the material constructs are not the whole story. Fashions would never occur in music if it were only a matter of these materials; rather some more subjective orientation toward them comes into play. Moreover, music has a sequential aspect wherein it is not merely a matter of what tones are experienced and retained in memory but in what order they are experienced.

Before proceeding to the aspects which are closer to the subject in the subject-oriented tension, one more point needs to be made about the material constructs. They exist as constructs, rather than as particular physical sensations in the central nervous system. One could be in an acoustically imperfect hall, or could be listening to an old recording of a historical performance, or one could even have hearing defects and still be able to experience the appropriate constructs. The minimal physical circumstance necessary is that the sonic problems not be so severe that they themselves become a distraction. The threshold at which they begin to constitute a distraction is itself relative; in the present age of stereophonic recording with high fidelity to the originary sounds and of auditoriums especially designed for concerts, the distraction threshold is probably much lower than it was in the past.

A second aspect of the awareness tension is that of the mental act of being aware. In this region the personal biography is punctuated by acts of apprehension. As one goes through a piece of music, one experiences it sequentially; there is a temporal character unique to a particular musical composition, but there is a unique temporal aspect to a particular experience of a particular composition. One can point to perhaps the first time one heard a given work and contrast it to a later time when it began to become a cliché or when it was first really understood in an interesting way. The attraction of music evidently depends upon apprehending actions of this kind. In previous sections we referred to this as the enacted or executant nature of music.

As important as the material constructs and acts of apprehension are, and as necessary as they are, we have not yet distinguished music descriptively from other sounds. Airplane engine sounds have material constructs; they do not sound "like airplanes" apart from our experiential constructs of them, and they have a temporal dimension to them wherein we may focus on a particular hearing of an engine or be taken up into the pulsating sound of one. Some people even make distinctions between different kinds of airplanes and their engines much in the way that they can identify musical compositions. Even those strange people who purchase recordings of airplane engines and play them through hi-fi systems, however, would not confuse their enthusiasm for musical enthusiasm. There is one more dimension that goes into setting the experience of music apart from other experiences.

There is an idea of music which is part of a mentality. Sounds which are not ordinarily taken in a musical way can be approached as musical by structuring one's receptivity with this idea — as much electronic music verifies. The idea of music is itself an orientational ultimate, much in the way that the idea of geometrical figure, of number, of vision, of right are ultimate ideas. By "ultimate" it is merely implied that one grasps them intuitively and uses them to define other experiences. One characteristic of this orientational aspect of music is that the mentality is oriented toward the acts of apprehension and the material constructs themselves. While other experiences have enacted and construct dimensions, the idea of music sensitizes one to the enacted apprehension and material constructs as the primary foci of attention. No experience is purely a matter of orientational ultimates, though math and logic come close; or purely enacted apprehension, though remembering comes close; or purely material construction, though inebriation comes close. However, different kinds of experiences are typified by different emphasis of and interrelationships among these different aspects of awareness. Musical experience seems to entail an orientational sensitization toward the enacted apprehension and the material constructs. The idea is to focus upon the mental construct of sensations and the enactment of them.

With the distinctions and conceptual hardware of this simple phenomenology in mind, it is easy for us to typify music in this manner. Indeed, we could go into a much more detailed account, though for what purpose would seem to be unclear. The average person composing, playing, or listening to music, however, does not think in such an explicit way. Indeed, most readers will have forgotten the distinctions made above by the time they have begun reading this paragraph. It is simply not the usual way of thinking to enter into a double epoche, suspending any concern with subject (ourselves) and object (our environment), and focusing on various aspects or dimensions of awareness. We have to work at it a while to think in such an unnatural manner. If music is a mode of experience structured by such a double epoche and typified by a particular mix of awareness modes, how do unphilosophical people do it? That is, how do they put themselves into a mentality when they are barely able even to articulate a description of it?

Humans are quite adept at using various kinds of symbolism to cue in mentalities which are only discussed with difficulty. These symbolic mechanisms take the form of conventions. By convention, commercials and fishing stories are not taken at face value. By convention, plays are distinguished from reality. Conventions accomplish in real life what epoches — suspensions of some usually-retained concerns — accomplish in philosophical phenomenology. Consider the rituals of a serious music concert, with the performers attired formally, shaking hands at certain moments, standing at certain times, etc., with the audience clapping at certain times, some of them dressing "up" for the concert. The rituals cue in the orientational idea of serious music without requiring that one be aware of the distinctions needed to even think about it clearly (see Kaplan, 1951: 134). Attempts to deviate from the rituals elicit sufficient dismay and hostility that it is obvious that they have some notable purpose, but most people do not venture to say what that purpose might be.

In performance it is important to master the objective realities, to subject them to habit, so that the full attention of the performer can be given to the apprehension and enactment of the material constructs. One account of an orchestra's rehearsal described it thus:

> Integration of the musical activity becomes increasingly a matter of meaningful gestures and of reliance on fitting one's part into an aural pattern. It is the latter which is all-important as the group becomes more proficient, so that it is commonly accepted among professional musicians that a first rate symphony orchestra will sometimes play well in spite of a poor conductor. (Kaplan, 1955: 355)

A similar account is given by someone who was in the process of becoming a reasonably accomplished jazz musician. He had to routinize the objective aspects before he could improvise, letting his attention become wholly absorbed into the executant and material construct aspects. This practice made improvisation possible (Sudnow, 1978).

Some would maintain that this had important implications for performance. With too much emphasis on the objective aspects, on the performance as virtuosity, for instance, the mode of communication between hearer and composer is disrupted. The occasion becomes a mere athletic performance. Similarly, with too much devotion to the orientational techniques, too much involvement in an exegesis of the score, the occasion takes on the aspect of a lecture-with-example rather than a performance. The primacy of the executant and material requires a delicate balance. The appropriate orientation intends precisely such a balance. If the balance is lost, the performance

> achieves a quality of self-consciousness, of methodological and critical clarity, which destroys the spontaneous and naive encompassing of the spectator by the work of art. The ability of the work of art under such conditions to cause the audience to suspend its awareness of all other worlds, and to enter into the work or world presented, is nullified. (Bensman and Lilienfeld, 1970: 115)

The performer is caught in a dilemma between showmanship on the one hand and archaeologism on the other. In conducting, Wagner began to assert interpretation over score, and Toscanini reasserted the primacy of score. Both efforts were undoubtedly needed in their time, in order to overcome literalism in Wagner's time and corruptive habit in Toscanini's. Both were single-mindedly concerned with maintaining the awareness tension appropriate for music, though it is unlikely that either one of them verbalized it in those terms.

The Case of Opera[14]

In the previous section music was described as occurring within an awareness tension, from which other realities, be they subjective or objective, would be distractions. It was also noted that the world of this particular kind of awareness tension was marked off from other worlds by conventions, especially by ritual conduct. Music as a mode of establishing communicative social relationships among composer, performer, and listener thus engenders a secondary social formation of ritual communication. That is, the maintenance of the conventions is itself a sociological phenomenon.

It has also been said that conventions serve the purpose of suspending one's mental involvement with certain realities and phenomena. These conventions parallel the phenomenological philosopher's epoches. What the philosophers do by way of a thought experiment for purposes of focusing on the phenomenon of awareness as awareness, many people seem to do as a matter of course in their musical conduct. For the duration of the performance, oneself and one's natural environment are set aside; their present relevance is suspended. This situation highlights the multiple realities in which the actor lives.

The intent of the present section is to illustrate conventions as epochs in opera. Opera is selected because the setting aside of some realities in order to maintain a delicate and complex balance within a certain fragile awareness structure is more obvious in opera than in other forms of musical conduct. Precisely because opera has so many conventions, because it differs in so many respects from the natural attitude in which an actor assumes that there are correspondences between the ideas of object-realities and the object-realities themselves, it is a difficult mentality to maintain. Many who master the apprehension of sophisticated music have no taste for the sophisticated apprehension required in opera. Moreover, the fact that operatic communication occurs in an awareness tension that is fairly remote from other realities has enabled operatic composers to address several audiences at once. Sophisticated opera may reach unsophisticated or even differently sophisticated audiences because it is a multi-message ensemble.

To begin with, opera sets aside all naturalist assumptions. It may populate its stages with mythical characters, impossibly heroic personages and dei ex machinae. Even when attempts are made to duplicate the appearance and sound of real settings, such pseudo-naturalism is part of an attempt to transport the spectator-auditor to a time and place quite remote from the naturally available world. Verdi's inquiry about ancient Egyptian music (he was told the ancient Egyptians used flutes and harps) led him to give *Aïda* an exotic flavor, i.e., one smacking of something beyond the lived world of the audience. And Puccini's research into the pitch of the bells of Rome and his securing a poem in local dialect would have only heightened the contrast between the plot of *Tosca* and any plausible sequence of events if he had been seeking to reproduce the lived world of his audience. Even in the midst of the verismo movement, where composers and librettists attempted to adopt the naturalist literary stance of Emile Zola and Giovanni Verga,[15] a true-to-life art form was not in the cards. The very suggestion that common people sing their conversations and launch into arias of their innermost thoughts would be absurd. Any parallel between real life and verismo opera must occur in some mode (e.g., within an awareness tension) other than an objectivist or descriptive account.

The successful opera departs from reality almost out of necessity. It focuses upon the experience of scenes, the creation of which requires supernatural intervention, immediate romances, and, most importantly, fateful ironies. Too extensive an elaboration of a more natural narrative and setting would detract from the scenic experiences per se. Thus the plots of operas often do not make good stories; sometimes they condense good plays which in turn would not make good stories. The spectator-auditor in opera is not to be led to focus on narrative — which is a form of referring to external reality in an objectivist mode — or description but to experience a number of scenes in a mode of presentation and reception which suspends any engagement in the natural structures of the objective world.

There is little character development in opera, compared to some forms of fiction. While there are memorable characters, they are projected in terms of the scene in which they are featured. The less complicated the personage, the more readily this can be done. In any case there is no gradual psychological unfolding of a biography; such a development would be too narrative and hence bring the distractive time structure of the everyday world into play. Moreover, it would have an objectivist descriptive nature which would violate the awareness form of opera itself. Plot, setting, and character may be emphasized in literature, but not successfully in opera. Opera captures a psychological state in frozen form, much in the way of Mona Lisa's smile, to be recalled in scene after scene by a few bars of music.

Moreover, the materials out of which the present entertainment of the audience could be constructed are not generally emphasized. The audience is part of the objective world, and each member of the audience is to himself or herself part of the subjective world. The entertainment of the audience, therefore, would be both an objective and subjective distraction. Thus even the music as a directly stimulating, interesting, or pleasurable experience must at times be set aside, or at least subordinated to the whole. This is why second-rate music may be found in first-rate operas, though there is no inherent reason why excellent music cannot be subordinate.[16] The particular talent of the opera composer is making listenable music seem appropriate in a non-concert occasion. The very interrelations of the scenic personages are revealed in part by a set of musical means unattainable to the mere world (Schutz, 1956: 233).

In transporting the observer-auditor into a surrealistic world where tragedy and comedy can be mixed (as in *Don Giovanni*) and conversation replaced by the extended recitation of simultaneous asides and successive soliloquies, opera takes the normal understandings of the social world and brackets them, puts them aside. It takes the social situation out of social time and interaction dynamics and places it into musical time and scenic construction dynamics. One who would apprehend it must transcend the structures of the everyday world as well. If one is to go beyond the musical enjoyment of vocal performances, which may be derived from musicals, songs, and oratories as well as from opera, one must de-emphasize even the performing which occurs in opera. In the way that a fluent speaker of a dialect does not take note of the pronunciation used by a fellow speaker of that dialect, one who apprehends opera as opera must go beyond the performing thereof. This is not to say that there is not a great deal of material for the opera critic to attend to — specifically, distractions in the form of unconvincing or flawed renditions — but there is a difference between the message of an opera itself and what can be ascertained from the opera critic's column which is devoted to it.

Schutz (1956) once described the genius of Mozart's operas and opera in general as the presentation of the social situation. That is not to be taken in the historical sense; Schutz explicitly rejected the idea that operas were meant to reflect historical reality. Whatever is reflected in opera is incidental to the main message of a given work — e.g., the historical implications of the theme of the rivalry between family loyalty and nationalism, a theme which is found in such works as *Aïda, L'Assedio de Corinto,* and *La Navarraise.* Who listens to *Aïda* to learn that nineteenth-century Europeans were exposed to the problem of divided loyalties? What Schutz meant was that the awareness of certain social situations is made present to the spectator-auditor.

What is left after the naturalism of the everyday world is removed is a drama. After all plot plausibility, character development, and narrative interest are removed, what is left is a performance. What is left after the consciousness of the performance as performance is removed is the experience of a situation. To bracket and set aside the natural world is to set aside objects, realities which correspond to but are not part of experiences. To bracket the elements of narrative is to bracket and set aside part of the noematic, enacted region. To bracket the witnessed performance as witnessed performance parallels the bracketing of the material constructs or hyletic givens. What is left is an awareness of the social situation, not consciousness of it as a descriptive category but the experience of such a consciousness as a genre of awareness. One gets taken up in the situation so unnaturalistically portrayed.

Opera is an interaction process between creators and audience. Composer, librettist, set designer, director, conductor, and performers develop a constructed presentation. Over time, this social construction may be received by presenters and audience alike as a given, a title in the "standard repertory," or it may be presented anew several times in a century in a "revival" of a less familiar work. In any case an interaction occurs between creators and audience.

The interaction is not precisely a communication, in the usual meaning of the term. Many of the lines may be lost behind the orchestral swells or uttered simultaneously with other lines. In the case of a performance from the standard repertory, the audience does not acquire a new message or gain completely novel experiences. Indeed, many may know the work well, or review it from printed and recorded material beforehand. The interaction occurs for purposes other than the communication of some content or message.

Humans experience social situations at the orientational level as well as at other levels; at the level of categorical *ideas* of the social circumstances as well as the existent circumstances to which such ideas may be directed. They know of humor as humor, irony as irony, shock as shock. With opera, they can renew such experiences without imposing impossible demands on objective social circumstances. With opera they can experience vengeance without perpetrating it, experience tragedy without creating one, and in the process they allow this particular kind of knowledge to mature. Opera, then, is a social interaction form which is structured and persists in order for humans to perform a particular cognitive function.

In an age of cinema and television, wherein pictorial authenticity comes to be expected by many, the improbabilities involved in opera present more difficulty than before. In an age when media do not leave much to the imagination, opera is at one and the same time apprehended with more difficulty and with a greater liberation from the tyranny of the trivial prose of the everyday world. Materially, cinema has outbid opera for spectacle while imaginatively it has underbid it.[17]

2
Participation in Music

I. ROLES AND MUSIC

Up to this point we have been describing those aspects of music by virtue of which it serves as a form of social interaction ("communication"). Because it unfolds its tones in "inner time," for instance, the form musical interaction takes is a mutual time flow experience on the part of composer, performer, and listener. Secondary social formations, ranging from the rituals and conventions used to maintain appropriate mentalities, to the property rights and obligations related to music, are contingent upon the realization, the enactment, of these interaction forms. Our account has stressed the historicity of music — its executant nature, the ad hoc character of its meaning, its relativity, the dialectical relationship between its changing meanings and constant aspects. This, of course, is only part of the picture.

Like much of social life, music is processual. However, people do not live in perpetual motion alone; they come to crystalize their conduct, to fashion it after typical stock meanings and stock routines. This is not to say that the historical natures of social life and music are nullified but that that very historicity engenders in people a yearning for stability. They know that their personal routines will be revised, they know that history will not stop, but they nevertheless make treaties with chaos, as it were. They structure their lives so that they can recall the recent past and say of themselves, "I can do that again," and of others, "There they go again." History itself then takes the form of a dialectic between the new and the familiar. The very actions which constitute history are predicated on expected outcomes, which themselves are predicated on memories; the new therefore depends upon the old because of this kind of routinization.

Social roles are stock combinations of interrelated actions, which bridge the past and the present. When someone enters a department store and takes on the role of customer, he or she will act in ways customers have been known to act in the recent past.

32

Then others — e.g., cashiers and stock clerks — will be able to say, "There he (she) goes again," and will know how to interact with the customer. The retailers are ready for the customers; they would lose business if they tried to control the customers, but they would also lose business if they were not ready for business-as-usual.

Within any given role there are types. Many an occupation has its stock knowledge of the types its members encounter. Retailers can speak of types of customers, as students can speak of types of professors. Similarly a given musical role, such as composer, has its types: the dreamer, the cosmopolitan, the ascetic mystic, the asthete, the master, etc. (Silbermann, 1963: 78). A role itself, therefore, is not fully descriptive of what goes on in the course of a role performance. The meanings and experiences which occur differ markedly from one composer to another, one oboist to another, one vocalist to another. The dialectic of sameness and difference, one and many, similarity and uniqueness, continues despite the routinization which occurs in roles.

In addition, roles are only one aspect of a person's structured existence. A given person has a sense of continuity within a stream of consciousness which is more closely identified with the person than mere roles. What happened to "me" before "I" was an oboist is a part of "my" life because of a biographical continuum which is "I" in a very personal and unique sense. If through some medical problem "I" can no longer play the oboe, that may be unsettling, but it would not be as disorienting as, say, amnesia. It would not be as disconcerting if what happens to me today will not have happened to me by tomorrow. In the loss of the ability to play the oboe, it would be a matter of "my" not having a role available to "me" any more, but "I myself" would not be destroyed and fragmented.

In some cases a whole host of social relationships which develop around a role becomes the social world in which one leaves tracks. One comes to know oneself and develop oneself by virtue of one's impact on others, and without leaving tracks in the world one does not know oneself. If one's engagement with the social world is largely musical, if one's sense of self is largely dependent upon the relationships attendant upon one's musical role, that role is obviously a significant part of one's life. It is, in such a case, likely to involve considerable psychic investment. In that case, the musical role is more than a role, it is a large part of one's identity. A considerable factor to take into account when examining a given person's musical role is to what extent the role represents the person's identity as well.

Roles always exist in the plural; for each role there is a reciprocal role. There is no customer without seller, no parent without child, no guest without host. In role relationships there is a division of expectations along reciprocal lines. In the case of musical roles, it should come as no surprise that different aspects of music are distributed unevenly across the different roles. The role of composer, for instance, involves more creativity than does the role of listener. What is interesting, however, is that what is emphasized for one role in one era is emphasized for a different one in another era; the public taste, for instance, was reflected in composition before the romantic era and in performance and attendance during and after it (Mueller, 1951: 10). Serious works were composed for the patrons on a regular basis in Mozart's time; they are played for audiences now.

In the eighteenth and early nineteenth centuries, notables' private patronage represented a conservative influence, while the marketplace represented a progressive influence; the situation is reversed today with nonmarket commissions sponsoring innovation and the market audience creating the continued demand for the classics (Adorno, 1976: 131-132). This reversal reflects the shift described above, with the performer's role enactment reflecting the public taste in a way that the serious composer's once did. Notice that what one role gains another loses. That stems from the very nature of role relationships, their reciprocity. Similarly the more the composer's role is accorded creativity, the less room there is for improvisation on the part of the performer. The more there is an assertion of will on the part of the performer, the more the audience must take a passive role. The more a composer's intent is followed, the less of a ham the performer can be. There are thus conflicts built into the very social form of music, conflicts between composer and performer, composer and audience, performer and audience, virtuoso performer and virtuoso conductor, etc. Such conflict is itself a form of interaction and should not be seen as the downfall of music. It is a commonplace among sociologists that conflict is a form of social organization, not a symptom of its absence (see Simmel, 1904).

Since the success of music depends upon a balance between literalism and capturing a public, a delicate maintenance of an awareness tension among a public but around the composer's material, the conflicts among the musical roles serve an important purpose. It is by virtue of the inherent conflictual nature of the social form of music that actors can strive for the requisite balance. If the social form were an expression of the meaning of music in the way that an ant colony is the expression of an instinct, there would be no room for actors to maneuver in order to establish the necessary awareness tension. But precisely because the social form of music involves roles which are ambiguous with respect to musical meaning, there is room for the mix of material and spontaneity appropriate for a given setting. Just as an election is a conflictual social form whose outcome is uncertain and hence meaningful, music is a conflictual social form whose outcome would be meaningless without an element of the uncertainty which goes along with conflict.

The social role is sometimes said to be the building block of society; this is obviously erroneous in the case of music, and it is less obviously erroneous but just the same wrong in other instances. The interaction and the attributes of the interaction are more fundamental than the roles involved (Sorokin, 1969: 39–41) and determine how the various roles will be played. In music, the nature of the interaction is such that the roles will be played out in a conflictual manner. This does not mean that psychic hostility and other unpleasantries commonly associated with conflict will necessarily be present — though they may be — but that cross-purposes and mixed motives will be a structured part of various role relationships.

II. THE COMPOSER

Composition exists as a role separate from other musical roles only in the West. In other societies music has either not separated itself from folk culture or has not developed a notational system that can be relatively specific with respect to the tone patterns to be produced. Traditional folk music, in contrast to the commercialized imitation of some folk music styles, is the work of the nonspecialist; it encompasses lullabies, work songs, ritual chants, and other musical phenomena which develop as part of the common lifeway of a traditional community. What is not handed down from one generation to another in folk music is the work of improvisation. In such a case, there is no composer as such, and hence no need for an elaborate notational system. Where there is a complex division of labor, as in the recent West, a notational system and a composer role can develop (Kasdan and Appleton, 1970: 50-51).

The cosmopolitan culture of the differentiated, complex modern society is not the only one which exists. Rather, the cosmopolitan culture ("big tradition") coexists with a number of localized, often lower-class subcultures ("little traditions"). For instance, the cosmopolitan Spanish-language culture of Mexico coexists with a number of Indian cultures and the American culture with various "ethnic" cultures. Thus folk religions and populist political movements occur in modern societies as well as in isolated, traditional ones. So too traditional folk music is to be found in the modern world; and sometimes mixed musical forms such as jazz, characterized by both specialist and nonspecialist musical forms, are to be found. In the case of jazz, composition is minimal or absent altogether, while there is specialization in performance (see Sudnow, 1978; Kasdan and Appleton, 1970: 52). The composer's role, which is part of the cosmopolitan musical culture, is thus absent from noncosmopolitan folk music and is marginal to mixed forms such as jazz.

The composer's role has some similarities to the listener's. It is a terminus of the social interaction rather than a mediation. While the meaning of the music is made present by the performer, it exists as coming *from* the composer and *to* the listener. The composer and listener both orient themselves toward someone else's enactment in the process of setting their own *mental* enactions into motion. In addition, both composer and listener are in a structural conflict with the performer; they increase their personal efficacy, their unique contribution to the musical mentality, at the expense of the performer's latitude of action. But these similarities between composer and listener do not make them "allies" (to continue the conflict metaphor); the composer is a specialist while the listener more likely than not is a generalist. The more advanced the composer's skills, the greater the difficulty with which understanding comes to the listener.

The conflict between the composer and the noncomposer seems to take the form of a dispute over expressiveness. The noncomposer is tempted to take music as an expression of some extramusical psychological state, while for the composer the flows, evolutions, or manifestations of the tones themselves are the matter of music. The issue often appears in differences of preference over whether music should express some emotion or recall some scene from nature. Composers who work in theater music — from opera

Shipping and Billing Instructions

1. Send itemized invoice in triplicate to:

   University of the Pacific Library

   Technical Services Department

   · Stockton, California 95211

2. Cite our order # with each item on invoices and/or correspondence.

3. Send latest edition unless otherwise specified.

4. Report on items which cannot be sent or which will be delayed.

5. On invoice, show library discount offered.

6. Send only one copy of the item, unless otherwise specified.

7. Return one copy of order form in book.

8. Do not send if price is substantially above our estimate.

9. Shipments must be insured or sent at Agent's risk.

10. Send hardcover if published unless otherwise specified.

to movie scores — have to face the issue most directly. They either use their music to develop subtly the conventions by which the natural attitude is set aside or they give in to the purely commercial demand of the theater that the music evoke some "mood" — excitement, sentimentality, or whatever.

According to Adorno (1973: 43) tonal music is full of illusion, illusions to the effect that separate voices are part of an entity. This illusion itself, he maintains, is extramusical. Thus, he saw Schoenberg's atonal music, which accords each voice and each tone equal value, as an assertion on the part of the composer of concern with the musical material itself, as opposed to an expression of tonal illusions. Schoenberg's music was thus more "rational" (i.e., illusionless), more concerned with confronting the tones rather than creating the illusory psychological effects. Whether or not Adorno was right about tonal structures themselves not being musical, the "rational" intent of atonal music reveals the struggle which is endemic to the composer's role. Adorno goes on to criticize certain well-known composers for surrendering to the enemy, as it were, for creating purely utilitarian music which is designed to accomplish effects. "Dramatic music . . . from Monteverdi to Verdi presented expression as stylized communication — as the representation of passions" (Adorno, 1973: 38). "Wagner is not only the composer who knew how to manipulate the impulses of the psyche by finding for them the most penetrating technical correlates, but further he is the heir of Meyerbeer, the showman of opera" (Adorno, 1973: 173).

Obviously, if a composer and other members of a society share a community of musical experience, if their musical languages, so to speak, largely overlap, then it is possible for the composer to use his or her music to convey extramusical meanings (see Nash, 1964: 38). It does not follow, however, that music which can be used in that way or even music that is used that way cannot communicate musical meaning as well. It follows only that innovative music which has not had the chance to be given extramusical associations is unlikely to communicate extramusical meanings. Moreover, in the United States and other complex societies the musical world is fragmented; different sectors of society "speak" different musical languages; thus any music, no matter how traditional or innovative, has some social meaning and hence can be used for the purpose of invoking extramusical meanings. The extreme of innovativeness, for example, can invoke a stance of retreat from the social world, withdrawal, a counterculture.

The contemporary composer in complex societies is faced with a dilemma because he or she cannot gauge a musical creation for or slightly above a general audience. There simply is no one audience, but many audiences. There is no unambiguous musical meaning when a work which seems trite to some is shocking and a bit much to digest for others. There will therefore be poor communication with a large sector of listeners. Since American compositional training is now less frequently characterized by private study in Europe and more often by formal, institutional study in the United States, contemporary American art music compositions seem to be addressed to a specialized academic audience and hence tend to exhibit an avant-gardism somewhat beyond the grasp of the general listener (Nash, 1964: 44, 47-48). Why not, if the general listener does not really exist?

The absence of an audience creates problems even for composers fortunate enough to earn a living without doing the kind of hack work which they find artistically distasteful. Craftsmanship suffers when one cannot hear one's work performed, and performance in turn depends upon a paying audience. Electronic music is one route toward circumventing this dilemma because no performer is involved (Nash, 1964: 55-56). Milton Babbitt took this to its logical conclusion: that the composer can do without the listener altogether. He made an analogy between music and other academic specialties which had become unintelligible to the average well-educated person (Kasdan and Appleton, 1970: 57). Of course, if the awareness tension between listener and composer is lost, if interaction no longer occurs, we may have something other than music as described in the previous chapter.

While contemporary music has become increasingly composer-dominated, performers and especially audiences have turned to the music of previous centuries by way of response. It has been maintained that early in the twentieth century the composers began to so clutter their scores with subtle instructions that performers avoided them (Kasdan and Appleton, 1970: 51). Audience tastes, the expense of contemporary works in rehearsal time, losses at the box office, and the difficulty of "atonal" music for some ears undoubtedly account for the continued dominance of the classical repertory in serious music and the present isolated position of the contemporary composer (Martorella, 1974: 305). When a modern form such as electronic music is aimed at an audience, film producers and record manufacturers serve as gatekeepers; sometimes they proceed at their own peril. In a celebrated case, Edgar Varese's

Poeme Electronique was commissioned by exposition officials from the Philips Radio Corporation for the Brussels World's Fair in 1958. Played through four hundred loudspeakers in a Le Corbusier-designed pavilion, it elicited terror, anger, and amusement from thousands of people daily for six months; incidentally, cases of enthusiasm were also noted. Nevertheless, the conflict between composer and noncomposer does not disappear but rather emerges in relations between the gatekeeper and the composer on the one hand and between the public and the gatekeeper on the other.

In one sense electronic composition requires more of the composer than does more traditional, instrumental composition. The composer cannot simply try out some structures on a piano with pre-given notes, leaving only the effects of orchestration to the imagination. Rather, the universe of pitch and coloration must be defined by the composer, and then the architectonic organization can be established within that universe (Malhotra, 1979: 111). This expansion of the composer's role, supplanting the function that musical history itself previously performed, requires a different listening role. The listener must become attuned to a new style of music with each new kind of composition the contemporary composers create. At best, most people develop an appreciation for one or two genres of music; the listener who is up to the demands of the contemporary art composers must become far more eclectic in taste. If cosmopolitanism entails transcending all cultural barriers, this particular development reflects cosmopolitanism in the extreme. Thus, as the composer role itself is a reflection of the differentiation and specialization which characterizes the modern Western world, the expansion of that role exemplified in electronic music and forms close to it reflects the modern form of culture even more.

There are a number of social consequences of this contemporary embodiment of the composer/noncomposer conflict. One of these is the establishment of a number of associations designed to promote the works and status of composers in what is perceived by them to be an unequal relationship with conductors, soloists, audiences, managers, and businessmen.[1] Another consequence is that, as a somewhat deviant occupation, the role attracts individualists. It requires an uncommon set of attitudes and predisposing personality traits to work in the face of social nonsupport, to assume a variety of side occupations for money while really pursuing composition as a life-ordering interest, and to engage in considerable solitary activity. The sketchy evidence that is available suggests that as children composers and composition students are likely to have been considered different by their peers and to have been relatively uninvolved in peer activities (Nash, 1957).[2]

The fact that the composers' creations reach fame or oblivion at the whim of noncomposers suggests that the relative isolationism of the composers, however understandable, may be self-defeating. Meaning systems intended for a restricted population provide only a limited, sectlike world in which to express oneself. Any wider prestige is thereby left in the hands of others, who decide whether or not to perform a work. The prestige of the composers thus derives from that of the person who performs the compositions and from irrelevant factors, such as how the composer makes a living, rather than from the qualities of the compositions (Bensman, 1967: 58). In this one respect, the lots of the serious art music composers and the popular songwriters are similar.

While the contemporary art music composer, exemplified by those who work in electronic music, represents assertiveness and role expansion on the part of the composer, with an accompanying isolation from the rest of the musical world, the contemporary popular songwriter represents the opposite. The songwriter is someone who has abdicated the better part of the composer role. To begin with, the songwriter's product is not a finished composition but a mere melody line with lyrics. It is placed into the hands of a willing publisher, who in turn subjects it to processing by music arrangers, recording producers, and musicians. The final product may differ markedly from the songwriter's original conception. Thus, the songwriters make no aesthetic pretensions and are not generally interested in the aesthetic concerns of serious music (Etzkorn, 1959: 17, 73, 89).

Rather than a solitary involvement with musical material and technology, the songwriter deals with publishers and attempts to anticipate the tastes of the prospective market. Technical expertise is not even relevant; the songwriter need only be able to invent a melody which fits a given lyric and to fuse the two into a unit, either by recording it on paper or on some acoustical device such as a tape recorder. Exposure to the musical public seems to be relevant to success, but most important is the persistence needed to wear down publishers' resistance. Despite the fact that publishers usually return unsolicited songs unexamined, one song must get through the opposition and become a "hit."[3]

The typical successful songwriter began writing at age nineteen and was first published between the ages of twenty-four and twenty-eight. There is thus typically a seven-year involvement in the social world of the business before any success is revealed. Entry into the business usually began at the urging of someone already in the business. Presumably the vast majority who try begin with no inside contacts and hence are not successful. Songwriters' friends are often in the music industry but are not usually other songwriters. The songwriter thus seems to begin in an unfavorable position and must depend upon the personal favor of nonsongwriters for access to the market; that access, of course, does not guarantee success. Once successful, continued success is not guaranteed; the typical successful songwriter originated only one hit — i.e., a song with 1,000,000 sales — in a career (Etzkorn, 1959: 28-32, 69).

While contemporary music composers find themselves somewhat at the mercy of noncomposers, popular songwriters appear to be in an abject and subservient position. Only in 1931 did they manage to form a Songwriters' Protective Association to counter exploitation by publishers, and its success has taken the form of a standard contract commonly used in New York City and Los Angeles (but not Nashville) recognizing the right to a share in all income derived from a work. Incomes are handled by several collection agencies: The American Society of Composers, Authors and Publishers; Broadcast Music, Inc., and SESAC (formerly, the Society of European Stage Authors and Composers). Users purchase a license to play or broadcast works listed in the agency catalogues, rather than use unlisted works, to assure freedom from any legal difficulties. Most income comes from fees paid by broadcast users, and they in turn conduct market studies so that they can broadcast whatever the market wants. The market in turn is primed by disk jockeys, who try new records out and sometimes push a record. Songwriters do not generally approach disk jockeys directly but rather maintain professional distance. The publishers and recording business personnel plug new records with the disk jockeys. The whole presentation of a creation is thus entirely out of the songwriter's hands (Etzkorn, 1959: 33-59, 106, 143-149).[4]

While the contemporary art music composer may represent total assertiveness in the composer/noncomposer conflict, and while the popular songwriter may represent total surrender, the film composer falls somewhere between these two extremes. Most film composers make no great aesthetic pretensions; however, they do act as craftsmen who possess a sophisticated expertise. Many professionals experience a conflict between client demands and professional role requirements, but because music is a communication which cannot be translated into the language of the inexpert the conflict continues even after the composer is completely willing to do whatever the film producer wants. The film producer simply does not know how to tell the composer what he wants. Thus the composer must negotiate his creation with other parties in a project even though the "other side" is dominant (Faulkner, 1978).

The successful film composer has a comfortable income, with financial security taking the form of a likelihood of future commissions. That likelihood is increased by honorary awards and by recognition among the circles of film producers. The film composer cannot, therefore, compose in isolation but must maintain necessary contacts and an image of professional plausibility. In order to please the clientele it is necessary to "read" the individual client — i.e., ascertain what the film producer's inarticulate expressions about the desired music mean (Faulkner, 1978: 103-104). The negotiation begins with a "spotting" session in which the producer and/or director view the film without scoring. Note that the film has already been made, and the score must conform to the film's structure and time demands; this contrasts sharply with the task of opera composers, who often make considerable demands on librettists. During the "spotting" session the composer and client(s) discuss the film, evolve tentative interpretations, and reach decisions about orchestra size, length of recording session, and time allocated for composition. The troubles occur during the preliminary presentations of the score, especially when the results do not match what the client has in mind. Having to abandon a score and begin again on a film is common (Faulkner, 1978: 104-107).[5]

The dilemmas of the art music composer, the popular songwriter, and the film composer stem from the very nature of communications expertise. Communications must be geared toward the competence of the persons receiving them, especially if the communication takes an executant form as music does. Expertise, on the other hand, implies a limited number of fully competent persons. Success depends upon a learning process wherein either the ignorance of one party or the knowledge of the other party are violated, compromised, sacrificed. None of the alternatives in such a state of affairs seems to be fully satisfactory.

III. THE PERFORMER

The music performer typically produces music from a written score; the process is one of translating notations into sound (the case of the jazz performer, described below, is an obvious exception). What happens in this process is not a simple copying of some sounds from the past, i.e., from the time of the composing of the music. The score on the musical page does not function like a library index card which points to an invariable text of symbols stored up in advance, but rather like a stimulus for the performer to produce an enacted text of symbols. A score is thus at best a link between two kinds of texts, the composer text of originary intentions and the performer text of reproducing sounds. The performer does not act in the same mode as an archivist, whose function it is to determine what symbols belong to what text and if possible determine whose text it is. Rather he acts as a re-producer, whose function it is to create anew.

It can be argued that merely to copy an original without any new creative deviation from a text is impossible. The act of copying itself introduces something foreign into the original. In addition, there are the time-bound meanings, the consequences of relativity wherein the passage of time itself creates meaning changes. Nevertheless, we may speak of a recapturing hermeneutic, where there is an effort to copy an original as exactly as possible.[6] While the original, copied historical reality is thereby made present in only an approximate manner, such hermeneutic nevertheless can give one an analogical knowledge of the original.[7] When seen as an act of consciousness, however, any re-presentation of an original is a reconstruction as well; it introduces new dimensions in the very process of translating it into the present.[8]

In the case of musical performance, that which is being reproduced is not an idea, an object of contemplation, which can be more or less accurately copied. That which is reproduced cannot be frozen, preserved, and transferred to another person.[9] The music is an external production and creation anew in the experience of an intended audience; it will be inherently and significantly different from the originary experience of the composer. Nevertheless this reproductive hermeneutic must be a "faithful" re-presentation. "Fidelity" implies that the re-presentation is connected to the originary text by being subordinated to it. This subordination is accomplished by an articulation of the score but does not imply a mere copying of the original (which is impossible).[10]

Besides technical capability, the subordination inherent in the reproductive hermeneutic presupposes an ethic of honesty and self-restraint. The interpretive activity is undertaken with a sense of responsibility. This is not such an issue in the visual arts, where there is no question of a second physical realization of the visual text; the one visual objectification stands through time. But in music and theater there are multiple physical representations of a work.[11]

Thus the score of a musical composition gives but a basis for the beginning of a process of intelligent penetration and re-creation. The performer's meaningful focus is not on the score, though the score is important insofar it provides limits beyond which an endeavor ceases to be an interpretation at all, but within which there is a wide margin for diverse readings (Hartmann, 1949: 424). The score should be appreciated in terms of what it does communicate — the limits of a musical discourse. Antiquarian attempts to imitate antique instruments and other endeavors to copy an original in all possible respects do not further the interpretation of the score and do not enhance the interpretive process in the sense of a re-creative hermeneutic.[12]

The question of interpreting musical notation is not simply a matter of degree, of there being more or less room for interpretation than in the visual arts, or of difficulty, of requiring more or less technical ability to interpret. Technical ability is an instrument, a preliminary requirement for interpretation (Lehmann, 1935: 167; Hanslick, 1881: 112-114). Subordination to the text is not a technical or practical matter but an artistic and lyric one (Hanslick, 1881: 112-114; Furtwängler, 1948: 35ff.). Even if performance were only copying the original, even if it could recover the inventive spontaneity of the original, even if all subsequent historical associations and influences could be set aside, and even if the performer could trade places with the composer and generate the original rather than interpret a score, it would still be impossible to act as a mechanical automaton, applying purely technical skills. The performer is still a subject who will individualize the performance by recognizing the music and rendering an intelligent re-expression. In other words, the performer is an artist whose cognitive and re-presentative competence is not merely technical or practical.

Reproductive interpretation transfers the meaning of the

score into a new and different dimension; the score's text is replaced and absorbed. But the meaning embodied in this new, performative text is transferred again into yet another dimension when it is communicated to the audience, where it achieves its final intelligibility. In terms of this final embodiment, the score serves only as a resource for comparison and control. The enacted performance and the musical experience received by the audience are linked to the score but do not have the same meaning.

To understand the peculiar character of reproductive interpretation in the theater and in the music hall, it is necessary to analyze the differences between what can be written in a script or score and what is intended to happen in the visual and auditory world.[13] The medium of script and score notations translates in a two-dimensional way the playwright's or composer's thought-objects, which were conceived of in one dimension — that of time alone.[14] A beat of music and a phrase in theatrical dialogue are not "written" to be read but to be heard and witnessed. They are not intended as thoughts occurring in the mind of a reader but as transitive actions reaching beyond the interpreters to an audience. This does not mean that the interpreter cannot read the script or score meaningfully but that such a reading process introduces a fundamental deviation from the original intention. This kind of notation is not like a novel, which is intended for a reader, or a naturalistic painting, which is intended for an onlooker (Hartmann, 1949: 439); rather it is an instrument for putting down on paper and preserving, a mediative device for the permanent objectification of the artist's creation. Interpreting script and score texts is a matter of dimension-retrieval; the original time dimension, in particular, must be reconstituted in a mental language of duration. This mental language of duration in turn culminates in the auditory-visual movement.

There is a long historical route that must be traced to locate the point at which the performer or interpreter role emerged. The division of labor in society had to advance to the point not only of there being music specialists but also to the point of there being a distinction between composers and performers. The performance speciality itself needed time to advance to the point at which conductors emerged, charged with the responsibility of bringing a large number of performers' contributions together into a single, coherent interpretation. The audience also had to develop to the point of appreciating this kind of endeavor, aided in turn by the clarificatory efforts of yet another specialist, the critic.

The musical interpreter is thus a creator; the interpreter creates in the temporal, enacted, dimensions, and that which is created is that suggested by the score in a mere two-dimensional way. The interpreter parallels the creative process of the composer, approaching the work not as dead remains but with a lively, self-absorbing, and sincere conviction of its vitality and coherence. The interpreter enters into a twin vibration, twin to the subjective totality objectified in the work. It is not a matter of an identical twinship, but only when there is a parallel creative involvement is there a mediation of the intended, correct meaning of the work, and only then can a new audience grasp that meaning (Furtwängler, 1948: 62–64); for it is a re-creation by a person that was intended. Even when there are "definitive" interpretations available through recordings or even through vivid memories, those interpretations need to be brought to life, as it were, in the same way as a score needs to be. Just as the original inspiration emerged in the workings of a whole person, and as a "definitive" interpretation emerges similarly, every new interpretation must also emerge in the workings of a new personality; an impersonal rendition, if it were possible, would introduce a tremendous change (see Furtwängler, 1948: 11, 28, 56ff., 71). Certainly the inspiration of the interpreter is restricted and subordinate, existing differently than did that of the composer, but it must be nonetheless inspiration. In this sense, the reproductive interpretation of music clearly differs from, say, historical interpretation.

Of course, to assume that all performers engage in an identical activity would be patently incorrect. Some assert their activity over any composer's activity, as in jazz improvisation, while others do not deviate from interpretation as such. Some abandon artistic concerns, focusing on craftsmanship or commercial appeal instead. Some of the important variations on the performer role will be described below; the accounts, however, will not exhaust the number of possible kinds of performer roles. The performers themselves well know that they have quite a variety among their ranks, and the different kinds tend to form mutually independent performer communities. One study of the musicians of the St. Louis metropolitan area found no less than eight local, self-sufficient performer communities: symphony musicians, classical chamber musicians, college music professors, university-based musicologists and music historians who perform rarities, a "New Music Circle" of experimenters with electronic and nontraditional sounds, church musicians, popular entertainment musicians, and band musicians (Etzkorn, 1976).

Jazz Performers

The role of the jazz performer has not been a static one through the decades of the twentieth century. The changes which it has undergone provide an array of possible forms which performance roles may take and thus serve as a good point of departure in examining the performance role in general. Fortunately, a number of sociologists have taken an interest in the social situation of the jazz performer over a good many years. Consequently there is a reasonably good set of observations and published insights to begin with.

The sociologist's interest in jazz may derive from any number of factors. One may speculate that a social science which attempts to stand outside the social world and take a critical look at it appeals to the sort of person who would take an interest in countercultural art forms in general, and jazz existed for some time as a countercultural musical expression. This may well be the case, but it does not guarantee that the sociologist's interest could be translated into sociological insight. There is another factor involved that makes jazz performance particularly susceptible to sociology as well as to the people who happen to be sociologists. Jazz is a musical form which highlights improvisation, and it is particularly ensemble improvisation which is eminently sociological. A group evolves an expression, negotiates a social creation. Such is the view many sociologists have of society itself.

For jazz musicians a song is not a finished composition but a succession of chords determined by an original melody. The melody is played once; then while an ensemble repeats the succession of chords the individual members take turns in improvising substitute melodies around the chordal structure. The technical requirements for proficiency do not come with general musical competence because the jazz "sound" requires a melody which has half step dissonant relationships with the chords of the original melodic structure; this requires extended practice on such scales in order to obtain appropriate finger solutions and develop meaningful mental Gestalten in that scaled universe (Sudnow, 1978: 2, 18-19, 25). A commitment to jazz music must precede this distinctive learning process; thus, the social reality of a specialized musical community to which one wishes to belong comes before the technical where-withall by which one may join it.

The very existence of the musical form therefore depends upon the existence of a jazz community to which one may aspire to belong. Entry to the ranks of jazz performers resembles the gradual entry into an informal group, in contrast to appointment in an orchestra. The beginner is allowed to play a tune or two, on the condition he gracefully make way for the experienced performer to replace him. It is not a mere matter of seniority; the community exists through the medium of stimulating improvisations, and a threat to the latter could threaten the community itself. Thus while it is necessary that beginners be given a chance, it is also necessary that the community be maintained through the continuation of the jazz music process itself (see Sudnow, 1978: 29).

The early sociological concern with the jazz performer developed when the role was considered "deviant" for whites, since it was not a part of their culture. What struck the observer was that a group of working-class white musicians were elaborating upon a black musical form and crossing the racial barriers common at the time. Their socializing not only broke with custom, but their music was associated with the vice-ridden life-style of the poor white underclass living among minority groups. Thus, the jazz performer was seen as somebody who chose to become déclassé out of a musical commitment. Only younger males tended to do such a thing; the accounts emphasize that jazz performers were usually young men between seventeen and thirty; their marriage rate was lower than usual for that age group and the divorce rate was higher than usual. They also showed a propensity for gambling. Wives tended to be undomestic types of women, according to the observers. The jazz performer lived as lavishly as possible, not saving for the future. His work led him to travel constantly, rarely playing more than thirteen weeks at one engagement. He worked nights at dance music, played jazz with friends after that, slept mornings, and rehearsed in afternoons. His friendship group consisted of other jazzmen (Lastrucci, 1941: 169).

It was obvious that the jazz performer preferred an uncommerical form of jazz rather than what he had to play for a living. He saw his exuberant improvisation as a creative art and commercial music as technicians' ware. He was most at home in the jam sessions after closing time in small cafes, with small groups of fellow jazz perfromers. The sessions consisted of "Chicago" style improvisations — alternating individual improvisations with the ensemble maintaining the chords — or "Dixieland" or "New Orleans" style collective improvisation. Either style demanded "both a rich fluency of musical ideas and a highly developed feeling for harmonic and rhythm teamwork." The jam session was the time of entry for newcomers to the informal groups; and since the commercial dance music left little chance to evaluate skill, it was a time to evaluate talent (Lastrucci, 1941: 170-171).

The jazzman's life-style left him in continual insecurity. Because the commercial dance music he played for a living required no great talent, he could not earn a permanent place through skill. Jobs, fads, failure, and success followed unpredictable turns of events. A youthful appearance was necessary for such employment, with obvious implications for the future. Meanwhile, an informal network of associates had to be actively maintained for job contacts (Lastrucci, 1941: 171). All this was particularly troubling because it was separate from his real interest — jazz.

While jazz performers, as they aged, left the active jazz scene for financial and family reasons, younger men took their places. Thus Becker (1951; 1953; 1963) approached the jazz performance role as an example of a stable deviant status. Jazz performers could come and go, but the deviant role would remain the same. Becker's observations, made in the late 1940s and early '50s, reveal little change from those made by Lastrucci a decade earlier, but things would not always remain the same. Change was to take place, as we will see below. A most interesting fact noted by Becker was that the jazz musician's preferences, which were in conflict with the preferences of the commercial audience, were giving rise to some explicit conflict actions. Becker phrased the situation in terms of occupational sociology. The jazz performer was an example of a "service occupation," which brought an expert into face-to-face contact with a client. It was inevitable that the two parties would have widely diverging ideas of the proper way the occupational service was to be performed. As Becker saw matters, the jazz performer's rejection of conventional norms and life-styles was an outcome of this musician/nonmusician conflict. The conflict also gave rise to segregation of the jazz performer from the rest of the social world, his ritually hostile comments about non-jazz enthusiasts, and his deliberately distinctive style of dress (Becker, 1951: 136-144).

The career alternatives of the jazz performer represented different resolutions of the musician/nonmusician conflict. A career was not identified with one or two institutional employers but with a series of jobs. These engagements were informally ranked by income, hours of work, and public recognition. A performer was hired by his friends or through their recommendations; this insured at least minimum competency in performance, since the friends did not want to be embarrassed. However, job success was inversely related to artistic orientation; the better the job, the more commercial the setting. Thus, the artistic-minded performer would have to forego the better jobs in order to concentrate on jazz playing. The result was that there were commercially oriented cliques of musicians and jazz-oriented cliques. Those who could not reconcile themselves to either inartistic success or artistic insecurity had to leave the musical profession. It is not surprising that families usually opposed their offspring going into jazz and professional dance music because of their anxiety over irregular jobs and an unconventional life-style. Stabilizing factors such as marriage tended to lead the musicians toward the commercial alternative (Becker, 1953; 1963).

In those days when jazz was considered a deviant form, an isolation from legitimate culture structured the lifeways characteristic of the jazz performer. The jam session exemplified this isolation; the participants were self-selected, and the repertory was determined by subculture standards. The odd hours and obscure nightclubs guaranteed removal from most audiences; and to emphasize the anticommercial stance in a commercial society, the only patronage tolerated was that of buying the band drinks. Theoretically, the jam session music consisted of free improvisation around the melodies and harmonies of traditional tunes, but certain introductions, cadenzas, clichés, and ensemble obligati became associated with certain tunes. These comprised a set of folkways which could be learned only by playing, since they were not written down anywhere. Thus, the jam session used forms which tended to exclude the musician who was not culturally already part of the jazz community. Though explicit critiques of performance were rare, the musical norms were reinforced effectively (Cameron, 1954). Certain themes turn up in the jazz community legends which point to an attitude of distancing oneself from the larger world. An unknown youngster from the sticks is invited to a jam session and astounds everyone with his playing — emphasizing that art comes from unrecognized sources. A group meets almost total failure before making it big — emphasizing that the hostile world might yet be converted, but meanwhile nonrecognition may be the reality (Merriam and Mack, 1960: 218–219).

The latter theme — that the hostile world might be converted to jazz — came true, at least in the sense that jazz itself came to be accepted as legitimate. In part, it may have been a matter of established society losing its legitimacy, for Stebbins found jazz musicians in the 1960s still less prosperous than commercial musicians and more likely to favor free love and drug use; on the other hand they were still more organized in cliques than were commercial musicians (Stebbins, 1965). Nevertheless, Stebbins found that jazz was becoming respectable through, of all things, an authoritarian institution like the public school (Stebbins, 1966: 197). By 1967 Becker was being criticized for having described the jazz performer role as deviant in 1963 (Harvey, 1967: 35). Fewer jazz musicians were encountering family opposition, and more of them were coming from the middle classes, sometimes from musically active families. The younger musicians were finding audiences interested in jazz, and they saw no reason to exhibit a hostile attitude toward them. The proliferation of clubs where only jazz was played eliminated occupational dilemmas which observers since Lastrucci had noted; moreover, jazz musicians were no longer idealizing antisocial conduct. Even the social isolation of jazz musicians had broken down. Not all this came without problems; the younger jazz musicians, for example, encountered racial problems in their ranks which the older generation had avoided (Harvey, 1967). Apart from that, the hostility most particularly the jazz performer's seemed to be that displayed toward non-jazz music; Stebbins (1969) described jazz musicians deliberately showing disinterest and displeasure when complying with requests to play non-jazz music.

Jazz has therefore experienced upward mobility; the occupational dilemmas it once posed have somewhat mitigated. It is still, however, a music form most naturally enacted in the jazz session, independently of financial or administrative pressures to please a large public. The more it is taken out of that kind of setting, the less it is true to its artistic standards. It simply loses its interplay improvisation form, its mutual to-and-fro communicative aspect when it becomes an audience commodity. Jazz survived decades of hostility and rejection, but can it survive acceptance? One may well suspect that any removal of the performer-listener conflict would undermine a form of conduct such as jazz playing.

Performers of Serious Compositions

While the jazz player may work his way into a subculture, eventually receiving recognition as a jazz artist by playing other types of jobs, the professional image of the serious composition performer is much more closely tied to professional engagements. He or she evolves a self-image as a professional by performing in frequent professional engagements. Winning competitions and receiving formal credentials help, but there seems to be no general substitute for performing for pay (Kadushin, 1969: 396ff.). Tied to a long period of training which most likely began in early childhood, considerable energy comes to be spent in "making it." The formation of a professional self-concept through the professional experience is the psychological counterpart to the first real step toward "making it." At the beginning of the career, then, there is ambition for a type of success which stands in contrast to the commercial success obtainable by the dance and musicians. Here success and artistic merit are assumed to go together rather than to be in conflict.

For the instrumentalist, career ambitions aim at a position in a top orchestra. In North America, that means one of a small field of five organizations: the Boston Symphony, the Chicago Symphony, the Cleveland Orchestra, the New York Philharmonic, and the Philadelphia Orchestra. There is a lower rung of respectable competitors comprised of twenty-four organizations[16] and a third level of numerous civic orchestras. Within each orchestra ambitions are directed toward the more highly ranked positions, particularly the first chairs (strings) or first men (winds). These section-leading positions are perceived to make greater artistic demands and to allow greater professional development. The pay is about double that of positions further back in the sections, and the first chairs and first men seem to have a monopoly on the better teaching jobs in any metropolitan area.[17] There is additional prestige in being included in the reduced orchestra for performing works calling for a smaller size or for recording records (Bensman, 1967: 58).

Since principal positions are rarely filled from within the ranks of the local orchestra, employment advancement usually requires geographic mobility. Moreover, the practice is to fill openings with young performers who are perceived to be on the way up. Thus it is the young who maintain high ambitions and who pursue opportunities in other orchestras. A common strategem is to move from a section position in a major orchestra to a lead position in a lesser-ranked one so as to be in contention for a principal position in a major organization. All things being equal, talent should win out in all this, but it is generally recognized that all things are not equal (Faulkner, 1973b; Westby, 1960).

Despite the fact that artistic and commercial success are not incompatible, it should be obvious that the talented musician is in for a great deal of frustration. The fact is that most artistically gifted musicians will not have satisfied their ambitions before middle age, and then it is too late. The ambitions thus come to be scaled down, for at this juncture musicians are trapped in an occupational and social position. Because their training has been so specialized other alternatives are not available to them. The professional performer's training was typically that of the conservatory, and even most social contacts have been limited to other musicians. The option of solo performing is entirely unrealistic, given the fact that the bulk of instrumentalists play in the strings and only about ten string players earn a living in North America as soloists (Westby, 1960).

Though social prestige is accorded to serious music and serious music performers, the musician is perceived as being somewhat different from other people. The natural tendency of the musician is to build a world made up largely of other musicians. It is not a particularly small social circle, since it includes several hundred people – more than most people's socializing group – but it has its obvious limits. This relatively inbred society has a common folklore which, together with musical subjects, provides considerable conversation material. Thus, musicians who have never previously met are able to find much common terrain. Once again, as in the case of the jazz performer, there is a separate social world quite marginal to other social worlds. Within that world, in addition to the prestige system described above, individuals and ensembles may be known for some specialized kind of music; their reputations may be tied to the interpretation of a particular composer or a particular school of composition. Obviously, the conductors, soloists, and ambitious instrumentalists are to be thought of in this light (see Bensman, 1967).

Among opera vocalists, where a star system operates, competition is even more evident. The many European municipal companies which once provided employment opportunities are becoming increasingly reserved for local talent. The major American companies, in contrast, are international – the Metropolitan Opera, the Chicago Lyric Opera, and the San Francisco Opera. There are smaller American companies with limited seasons and an array of university productions of esoterica. Intense competition over limited positions isolates the performers in a way that does not seem to occur among instrumentalists; fees, contracts, and colleagues are not matters for open discussion. The secrecy naturally results in rampant rumors and gossip (Martorella, 1974: 93, 351).

The general life situation of the musical performer seems to stand in contrast to the pleasures of music itself. For the majority, artistic ambitions come to be regarded as youthful irrationality. Many would get out if they could. One researcher, using a life history technique, reports a statement of one musician about her children that is very revealing: "They are about the smartest, cutest, sweetest, and most artistic children in the world. They will be the finest of American citizens some day, but, we hope, not musicians!" (Kaplan, 1951: 313).

Conductor and Orchestra

While serious music itself is an interaction among composer, performer, and listener, and while orchestral performance involves an interaction among members of the orchestra, the relationship between the conductor and the performers is a supreme example of dialectical process. The work of the conductor is supposed to be one with that of the other performers, yet it is directed to them. The result of the conductor's efforts is supposed to be music, but the conductor does not make musical sounds. The conductor is clearly an ally of the other performers in the conflict with nonmusicians, but the conducting is designed to produce a desired percept on the part of the audience. Again, the conductor is clearly a performer, but the intent behind the conducting is articulated closely to that of the composer. The role of the conductor is fraught with contradictions.

The margin of freedom between what is specified in the score, on the one hand, and what is humanly possible to effect, on the other, is quite wide. The performer has considerable latitude in the rendition and can therefore make a given composition sound any number of different ways. In the early eighteenth century, improvisation was not only tolerated but called for, especially in operatic music. The bass part was written as a framework, and the players and conductor filled in the harmonic material in accord with numerical figures. At first, in the seventeenth century, notation was employed to allow different instruments to duplicate the bass material at intervals specified by the numbers, but inevitably improvisation upon the duplication came to be expected (Kaplan, 1951: 172-173). As composers came to be increasingly specific about what they wanted, in accord with a developing body of musical theory, the tradition of performer creativity came to be directed at realizing various potentials within a score, particularly along lines in accord with the composer's intent. Thus, the issue of right and wrong, poor or excellent interpretations of scores arose.

When a performer reads ahead in a score to anticipate the bodily preparation needed in a passage, the score is being translated into a personal body language which is identified by the sound it is expected to produce. This language is more efficient than the theoretic language of the scholar because it shares in the executant nature of the musical meaning itself. A conductor, unlike other performers, has no automatic linkage between body language and the sounds to be produced; yet the body language of the conductor cannot be entirely personal. The conductor must anticipate the desired musical meaning and communicate that to the other performers, who after all know their own body languages best. To have any effect, the conductor must, as it were, become part of the score which is read by the other performers. The conductor becomes that aspect of the score which marks the developmental flow of the music.[18]

The signs used to "mark" the flow of the music are arbitrary in the sense that they have no intrinsic connection with their corresponding meaning, just as different languages use different words for similar meanings. The signs of language, however, are agreed upon by a language group. *Marks,* in contrast, are biographically specific for persons who use them, and they exist only within the terrain which one can personally influence (see Schutz, 1973: 308ff.; and 1972: 116ff.). The signs which comprise the musical score are insufficient for purposes of performance. Hence the conductor must use his or her own marks, but rehearsal time needs be spent with the orchestra so that these marks cease to be merely personal but become marks for the other performers as well. The biographically specific experience of making certain motions indicators of a musical meaning is the objective of rehearsals; it is through such experience that coherence ("control") is achieved.

The rehearsal is therefore itself a form of interaction separable from the complete interaction among composer, performer, and listener.[19] In the case of entirely unfamiliar scores or amateur performances, it may begin with a concern for getting the score itself right, and the rehearsal may be punctuated with social conversation, but usually the closer it gets to its objective the more the concern is the musical meaning itself and the exercise of appropriate control (Kaplan, 1955). The establishment of marks is paramount and works to the exclusion of intellectual concerns which stand outside the musical flow itself.

> The talking kapellmeister becomes suspect as one who cannot drastically concretize what he means; also as one whose chatter prolongs the detested rehearsals. Aversion to talk is something orchestra musicians have inherited from manual laborers. (Adorno, 1976: 110)

The challenge for the conductor is therefore not simply one of the intellectual mastery of the music and a grasp of the desired outcome but also establishment of personal dominance over the rendition of the orchestra members. This is aided by the ritual embodiment of authority that goes with the role, but the conductor must nevertheless accomplish in the short rehearsal time what politicians have spent lifetimes attempting. This is a problem for the orchestra members as well as for the conductor; they know that the artistic standards which they value depend upon the coherence which the conductors should be able to effect, but they are themselves artists who value their freedom and have confidence in their expert control over both their body language and instruments.

> The orchestra's attitude toward the conductor is ambivalent. . . . Its members want him to hold them on a tight rein, but at the same time they distrust him as a parasite. . . . (Adorno, 1976: 110)

It seems that the success of the conductor can at times be associated with as much resentment on the part of the orchestra members as can failure.

> The musician regards the conductor as an arbitrary, capricious martinet whose knowledge of music is eclipsed by his egotism, megalomania, and flair for histrionics — qualities he can indulge to the fullest when he ascends the podium. (Bensman, 1967: 56)

Failure takes the form of making the orchestra sound bad; an old adage has it that there is no such thing as a poor orchestra, only poor conductors. The conductor's motions may be ambiguous altogether, and not serve as markings for the other performers. Or the conductor may indeed be able to communicate the desired musical meanings but may be simply unable to decide what is in order (Faulkner, 1973a: 150).

The conductor's authority is thus not simply one of knowledge, though that is necessary, or of hierarchical authority, but is a constructed authority based upon clarity, consistency, and enacted control. The ultimate embodiment of such authority is in the music itself. It follows that if the authority can only be embodied in the enacted medium itself, it can only be established if exercised. It is to be expected, then, that it will be tested; it needs testing. Resistance on the part of individualistic instrumentalists, purposeful errors to see whether the maestro can tell the difference, and nonverbalized negotiations over how much leeway the conductor will allow are concomitant to the process of the conductor establishing authority. It is a form of conflict, but when the result is music rather than a collection of notes it is because the instrumentalists both understand what the conductor wants and, rather than merely complying, they enter into the resultant music with enthusiasm. In short, the collection of legendary skirmishes between players and conductors, the elaborate typologies players have about conductor behavior, the paired reactions of resentment and respect, are all a necessary part of establishing the collective yet individual experiences which are necessary for better-than-mechanical renditions of music (see Faulkner, 1974).[20]

Because radio and recordings make the listener's exposure to the repertory more frequent, the effect of the conductor's efforts is highlighted. This tends to make the conductor a star and deprive the orchestra members of the credit they often merit. It might be argued that the music itself should be the focal concern, but for better or for worse, instead of an ever new repertory without rehearsals, as in the days of Mozart, now interest most often rests in the presentation of established repertory. Interpretation and interpreters become the variables and the focus of interest in many concerts (Mueller, 1951: 318). The same phenomenon which has worked to the contemporary composer's disadvantage has placed greater emphasis on the performance role, particularly that of the conductor. The conductor especially must bridge the subtle nuances of a mind of perhaps two centuries ago, while thinking in terms of a meaningful presentation of those nuances to a contemporary audience. In other words, "the music itself" does not really exist except as presented. The fact that there are different schools of conducting merely complicates the matter further.

An extension of the conductor's role which is peculiar to the modern world is that of editorial responsibility for the final result of recording sessions. In the earlier days of the recording industry the conductor would make a first recording, review it while the orchestra took a break, and then record the work again while adjusting the directions given to the players in such a way that the desired balance would be perceived on the recording. That meant conducting for a sound somewhat different from what was heard directly by the conductor in live performance. In live radio broadcasts and in the early television broadcasts, the knowledge of where the microphones were placed and a great deal of intuition and experience were all that the conductor had to work with. Sometimes modern listeners have difficulty realizing the special knack that recording conductors had to have prior to high-fidelity recording technology, particularly multi-channel magnetic tape. In more recent times the performance is recorded through many microphones onto multiple tracks. The tracks are then blended together to make two or four (stereophonic or quadraphonic), with appropriate adjustments and even dubbings made after the actual performance. The conductor, in consultation with the record company manager and the technical expert, supervises the blending process. The imporatnce of this kind of activity is that the conductor is doing physically what conductors have always done mentally — taken the role of the audience as well as that of the performer. The conductor must understand what musical meaning will be perceived by another and make adjustments appropriate for bringing about the desired meaning.

It should come as no surprise that the different schools of conducting are reflected in different schools of recording. Some conductors see to it that the full texture of a composition is clearly exposed in the recordings, while others order the balance to highlight one or two parts, with some of the material serving at best subliminally. Unlike orchestras, the electronic media is not too resistant.

Studio Musicians

From the perspective of symphony orchestra musicians and jazz performers, "going commercial" seems to represent a surrender of artistic concerns and, at best, requires some level of craftsmanship. Such a view prevails, of course, from the outside looking in. That view has its consequences for the commercial musician, who may or may not be concerned with the "art" in the work. From the inside, however, craftsmanship may be a point of pride which can support an image of professional accomplishment as effectively as can aesthetic claims. Indeed, craftsmanship is closer to the effort of the performer than art often is, because art is more an issue for the composer.

The studio musician must be a craftsman above all. The role may demand "dirty work," requiring little talent in the early phases of a studio career. However, technical prowess, excellent sight-reading ability, and familiarity with a wide range of musical styles comprise the minimum requirements for career success.[21] The studio musician, often on short notice, plays the full range of cinema music, television music (both live and taped), record dates, advertisement jingles, and even occasional sound effects. Prior to the studio career the performer may have belonged to jazz groups, big bands, symphony orchestras, concert stages, or any other less lucrative musical operation (Faulkner, 1971: 15, 6).

The conflict between commercial and artistic orientations, which bedevils and sometimes impoverishes the jazz performer and the symphony instrumentalist, appears in a most unusual guise in the case of the studio performer. In order to survive as a regular in studio work one has to have perfected a level of skill through a previous career of demanding musical work. Having "failed" in an artistic career thus becomes a normal channel into studio work. It is not so much that talent is unnecessary but that experience is crucial. In many cases the musician's childhood training and initial ambitions were focused on solo concert work. And often the frustrations of either orchestra work or the jazz life gave rise to a disenchantment which led the typical studio musician away from art work. In addition to these factors a period of "dirty work" in hack jobs often precedes success in studio works. Thus the studio performer is usually a person who has had to make difficult psychological adjustments through a multi-careered adult life. The art/commerce conflict remains very much in evidence under the form of psychological ambivalence about one's occupational past, one's accomplishment, and one's ambitions (Faulkner, 1971: 53–79).

"Dirty work" includes playing teenager dance music for records and hack music for television shows. Such undesirable engagements require little skill, involve tasteless music, and give rise to monotony. Success takes the form of frequent involvement in movie work, which may entail more interesting musical scores and more diversity. Entry into the inner circle of regular studio performers comes by way of sponsorship; somebody already in the business cashes in on favors and manages to get a job for the person being sponsored. Once in a job, assessment by colleagues is critical. Sponsoring is done reluctantly because the sponsor's reputation is at stake, and a respected performer may have to be passed over in order to make room for the newcomer (Faulkner, 1971: 156-157, 97-102).

New York City, Nashville, and Los Angeles are the three main centers of studio work in North America. Within the 32,000 members of the New York City musicians' union local (including many amateurs who might play on a weekend for a little extra money), a core group of nearly three hundred performers comprise the studio regulars. Slightly over a hundred of these are on the staffs of the three major broadcasting networks. The remaining two hundred are employed largely in theaters. Nashville has a core group of forty or so, out of six hundred local musicians' union members; employment is largely found in the recording industry. Smaller clusters are associated with recording studio work in other major metropolitan areas. The situation is somewhat unique in Los Angeles and Hollywood because film and television work, in addition to the recording industry, dominate the scene. Some three hundred performers comprise the core group in Los Angeles and Hollywood (Faulkner, 1971: 15-17).

The Hollywood studio orchestras, for which performers worked on a contract basis, dissolved in 1957 after a prolonged contract dispute. Hiring is therefore done on a free-lance basis for each engagement or series of engagements by musical contractors, who depend on their informal knowledge of available talent. The optimal occupation situation for a performer in such an environment is to have first-call agreements with several studios. The performer agrees to take "calls" when notified at least ninety-six hours in advance. The studios are motivated to maintain a number of such agreements because they want access to the better musicians; they cannot afford unnecessary re-takes during recording sessions. Because they have their own lists of performers with whom they are most comfortable, conductors and composers sometimes disrupt a studio's loyalty to its regulars. Section leaders are selected first, and they sometimes influence the selection of section members. All the bargaining, establishment of loyalties, and intrigue focuses on the music contractor. Only the rates of compensation are negotiated between the industry and union representatives (Faulkner, 1971: 22, 43–50).

The free-lance system leaves the performers exposed to a number of problems. Shifting fads in audience demand precipitate show cancellations and style changes, so that the employment situation is perpetually fluid. Films may be expected to feature an entirely different array of instruments from one year to the next. This can be expected to create anxiety in the ranks of the performers. Moreover, the quantity of available work varies when the different metropolitan areas compete with one another more or less successfully, and thus one's loyalty agreements with contractors vary in value. Moreover, the music departments in the companies compete with other departments for budgetary support. The performer simply has no control over all of this. In addition, one's skills may be misused or underutilized in any one job; status within the playing group remains as real a factor as in the symphony orchestras, and the oversupply of musicians makes competition perpetual (Faulkner, 1971: 18–20, 7–8).

Recording cinema music is perhaps the extreme form of studio music. Most "studio music," as the term is used here, is timed to match some action. In the case of movie music, the timing is brought to a precision which is hard to imagine in other musical settings — one tenth of a second. Sometimes the music may be performed at the pre-production stage and then dubbed into a film or video tape; it may not have even been composed and played with such a use in mind. However, the music of most concern to the studio musician is that played at the post-production stage. The composer has designed the score to fit a time structure that has been determined by the script and the acting staff. A copy of the film is marked with indicators which can be projected simultaneously with the playing of the score so that the conductor can conduct from the running visual film as well as from the written score. Hence there is something of a visual metronome. Additional markings are electric clicks generated by the film or tape and played through earphones worn by the performers. The instrumentalist thus has the score, the conductor, visual cues and earphone cues, as well as colleagues, all providing information (sometimes conflicting information) simultaneously. The level of craftsmanship required in such a process should be evident. Several good "takes" are made of each section of the score, after a once-through rehearsal. If the musician wants to hear the final product after the technicians have processed it, it is a matter of buying a ticket and going to the movies, purchasing a record, or watching television (Faulkner, 1971: 31-43). The product has been abdicated, alienated to a corporation, along with any control over its character or use.

The Youth Band Performer

Twentieth-century industrial societies have seen the emergence of semiprofessional youth performance groups. The performers tend to have informal training at best, and most of the income derived from their performances goes toward the purchase of instruments and amplification equipment. Thus they seem to be motivated more by a desire for social recognition than by the income. Most of the groups disband when their members are aged nineteen to twenty-five, while a few successful ones persist and become fully professional. The groups whose members attend college tend to last longer than those whose members do not. Group disintegration usually begins with the marriage of an important member, or an entry into some kind of employment that is symbolically or practically incompatible with further participation. On the average, members are involved from age fifteen to nineteen; most of them are male (Blaukopf, 1974: 17-18).

In general, the youth groups imitate the professional groups whose productions are disseminated through the mass media. The youth group repertoire is derived from the mass media, and their rehearsal involves listening to the radio or phonograph and trying to reproduce a professional group's "sound" (Blaukopf, 1974: 18). The groups may thus be seen as allies of the professionals associated with the mass media, plugging their product not only at no cost to the professionals or to the commercial corporations, but sometimes at great personal expense. On the other hand, the youth groups may be seen as part-time competition for local professionals, greatly depressing the employment prospects of local full-time performers.

The youth groups often begin with some innovative intent, but the imitation of commercially successful records soon becomes necessary when money is needed. Loudness is sought by these groups, even when the electrical equipment used distorts the sound; in fact, distortion is sought ("antifidelity"). Perhaps the "sound" of a professional group overextending its equipment to reach large crowds of people is what is being imitated. Thus, the electric equipment itself is used as an instrument rather than as a mere means of propagation; performers even practice distorting their shouts into the equipment (Blaukopf, 1974: 18-19, 21).

The groups appear in all the industrial societies, especially in North America, Europe, and Eastern Europe. The phenomenon is particularly striking in a country like Hungary, where the electric equipment needed may cost as much as the average year's earnings of a skilled wage-worker; in addition, an automobile must be purchased to provide the necessary mobility to keep engagements (Blaukopf, 1974: 20).

Dancers

It is a commonplace among the Marxian sociologists that social divisions and inequalities in the society as a whole create a situation wherein individual members of a class or group work against one another. The Marxians observed that a social arrangement in which the profits of industrialists depended upon a class of workers who were paid less than management, made the workers compete against one another. The worse-off the workers were as a class, the more desperate they became, the more they could be tempted to act as strikebreakers or to undercut one another's pay scale. Since the work could be done more efficiently by the young, child labor was common, throwing family heads out of work.

The situation of the dancers resembles in some respects what the Marxians were talking about. There is a large division between dancers and nondancers, with very limited opportunity available for the dancers. The dancers thus enter into intense competition, preventing any real group organization or solidarity. In addition, the art form requires youth, but the problem with this is that careers end at age thirty, rather than that child labor is involved.

The great divide between dancer and nondancer occurs informally in most cases, though educational institutions play a role. For males, teachers and coaches seem to provide the motivation to begin ballet lessons; for females, parents and physicians provide the necessary influence. Consequently females are likely to begin before age ten, while males tend to begin in their late teens. The informality of the training — a result of the individualistic competition which characterizes dance — leaves the dance student with no guarantee that the instruction is competent or likely to climax with entry into a professional career (Federico, 1974).

The student dancer typically has money problems. Rather than instilling a sense of realism, that condition seems to correspond with the dancer's reluctance to face up to the fact that any career would end soon after age thirty; only a few look beyond the dancing years to second careers in teaching or choreography. There also seems to be a reluctance to face the difficulties a career would create for a home life. An issue which the student dancer does seem to face squarely is a conflict with the teen culture. The dancers feel more mature — at least culturally — than their peers; they seem to carry their rejection of the popular culture into their young adult years, when they evince dissatisfaction with middle-class culture. Despite this, they do not seem to band together in a dancers' counterculture (Ryser, 1964).

The oversupply of recruits and the limited number of available openings in dance companies, together with a recruitment process lacking a certification procedure, leaves politics and luck as important factors in determining career success. "Such politicking runs the gamut from dispensing sexual favors to being willing to do extra work or even returning part of one's pay check" (Federico, 1974: 254). Luck takes the form of other dancers' illnesses and tragedies, conflicts between directors and other dancers, and one's own intrigues in discrediting another dancer.

Only four prestigious ballet companies, capable of providing satisfying careers, are available in the United States: the American Ballet Theatre, the New York City Ballet, the City Centre-Joffrey Ballet, and the Harkness Ballet. Research suggests less satisfaction on the part of performers in other companies (Sutherland, 1976).[22]

The Troubadour

In medieval times in southern Europe it was assumed that poetry was meant to be sung. It was a much more popular art form than it is today, with the jongleur or minstrel chanting the poetic verses of the day to the accompaniment of a viol or lyre. Festive occasions were graced by the minstrels who sang their chansons de geste, songs, and romances. They also told tales, played a variety of instruments, danced, juggled, and performed sleight-of-hand tricks. The role was evidently less specialized than that of the professional musician of today.

Accounts of the jongleurs go back centuries. They are known to have convened in the year 1,000 in Normandy, and they met together regularly during the slack season of Lent, when their public performances were forbidden. These meetings served as occasions to learn one another's tricks, techniques, and repertoires. The earlier jongleurs were not of noble birth but were nevertheless patronized by the nobility. By the thirteenth century, the practice of holding songfests was common in Europe. Apart from some cryptic lettering, the music of these traveling entertainers has been lost, though the words have often survived. One may surmise that the music must have been simple, for it to be recalled without any advanced notation.

IV. THE LISTENER

When music is viewed as a form of social interaction, the composer and the listener are at the termini of the process; the music begins with the composer (or performer, in the case of improvisation and interpretation) and ends with the listener. This does not mean, however, that the listener is merely a passive receptor. The composer and the performer typically orient their actions to the listener, structure them around the listener's response, or even assertively attempt to bring the listener around to their point of view. In that sense they are influenced by the listener.

The listener gives the professional status as well. Even when a composer or performer is oriented to other professionals, the latter take on the listener role. The musician becomes a professional only when listeners take the music to be professional. In addition it is the listeners who join the opera guild, support the symphony drive, attend concerts, buy recordings, and otherwise engage in conduct which establishes professionals or organizations of professionals as providers of a desired service. In turn the listeners often derive prestige from attending such musical events. This activity ranges from the symphony patron maintaining an image and self-concept as a cultivated person, to the teenager making it obvious that the "right" music is identified with her (Bensman, 1967: 55–56). Sometimes the artistic prestige sought by listeners forces the professionals to either upgrade themselves or be replaced.

When examining listener conduct, it is necessary to take account of both opportunity structures and personal stances. People who have had no exposure to sophisticated music because of poverty or cultural isolation illustrate the unfortunate side of the workings of opportunity structures. People who select one or more kinds of music from an array of available alternatives

illustrate the workings of personal stances. The opportunity structures are not determined solely by the economic resources; in
Moscow the necessity of having political connections to get music
and theater tickets and the government's policy of using the arts
almost exclusively to present Russian classics over and over again
to tourists combine to isolate Muscovites from current developments in art music (Robinson, 1980). On the other hand, the personal stances of the would-be listeners may reflect a response to
the opportunity structure rather than the independent choice of a
person who is informed enough to make a cosmopolitan decision.

A 1972 New York State study showed that some 34 percent
of a sample of the general public attended a concert or opera performance at least once during that year, of whom 51 percent were
in the $15,000 and above income bracket and 55 percent were
college educated (National Council of the Arts, 1973: 50). Social
class ranking, as reflected in income and education, thus seems to
be a factor influencing the listener role. Age is another factor; one
need only listen to radio disk jockeys to learn that different stations aim at different age groups, and that different kinds of music
are found on different kinds of stations. One survey of some
American college graduates showed that preference for classical
music increased steadily with age and that preferences for various
other kinds of music (e.g., folk, motown, rock, jazz) peaked
among people aged twenty to twenty-two years (Denisoff and
Levine, 1972). These patterns are not unique to the United States;
a Dutch study found interest in pop music decreasing with age and
interest in serious music increasing with level of education
(Volkman, 1974).

There is no intrinsic reason why social class ranking or age
should correlate with specific levels or kinds of musical listening.
People earning less than $15,000 in 1972 could afford a concert
ticket (as opposed to a color television or a series of movie tickets),
and twenty-one-year-old ears can hear as much in serious music as
can twenty-five-year-old ears. The relationship between such factors as class ranking and age is an indirect one whose nature is not
readily revealed through audience-study percentages.

The indirect relationship between people's "place" in the
social process and their musical conduct was considered at length
by Theodor W. Adorno. He observed that society existed as a
process in which different categories of people emerged because
the people in question experienced different life situations. People
made their way in the world in organized routines of conduct

which placed them in typically recognized categories. Musical tastes and practices fit in with the particular style of people's lives. Thus the musical routines found among different categories of people may not make musical sense but may still be understandable when seen in the light of their everyday activities. One can understand why a harried low-level business manager, for instance, may prefer "beautiful music" or "easy listening." The life situation does not "cause" the musical taste, but the two complement one another and form a larger whole that might be called a way of life (see Rose, 1978: 103).

Adorno described eight kinds of listeners. First, the expert is one of a relatively small number of persons. The expert spontaneously follows the course of music, hearing the sequence, hearing the past and future moments together with the present, even in complex works. Each sound is heard as part of a crystalized meaningful context. Next, there is the good listener, who also

> hears beyond musical details, makes connections spontaneously, and judges for good reasons, not just by categories of prestige and by an arbitrary taste; but he is not, or not fully, aware of the technical and structured implications. Having unconsciously mastered its immanent logic, he understands music about the way we understand our own language even though virtually or wholly ignorant of its grammar and syntax. (Adorno, 1976: 5)

Third, Adorno spoke of the culture consumer, who focuses on performance virtuosity of familiar moments of recognized pieces. These, he maintained, comprise the mass of concert-goers. Fourth, there is the emotional listener, for whom music is a psychological trigger. This type, says Adorno, prefers music like Tchaikovsky's, which has obvious emotionality. Fifth is the *ressentiment* listener[23] who cannot abide the excesses of various musical movements and who cultivates a suborthodoxy of unemotional Bach purity. Similar to the *ressentiment* listener is the jazz fan, who allows for emotion and mimesis using jazz as an alternative to that from which he is inhibited. Seventh is the entertainment listener, who is the object of the culture industry. For the entertainment listener music becomes a comfortable distraction.

> The structure of this sort of listening is like that of smoking. We define it more by our displeasure in turning the radio off than by the pleasure we feel, however modestly, while it is

playing. . . . If the culture consumer will turn up his nose at popular music, the entertainment listener's only fear is to be ranked too high. He is a self-conscious lowbrow who makes a virtue of his own mediocrity. (Adorno, 1976: 15-16)

Finally, there is the category of the musically indifferent, the un-musical, and the antimusical.

What Adorno did with his typology was outline some alternative motives or intentions which are or could be embodied in acts of musical listening. From these motives he proceeded to focus on typical motives which enable one to fit into the larger social world but which are too demeaning to be put into words. For example, any class society, in which only a few are well-off, exists by convincing the not-so-well-off either that they are inferior and do not deserve more of society's goods or that they can yet someday be counted among the few. While most people would not say in words that they are inferior, entertainment listening can accomplish the same psychological feat in a much more palatable manner. Others can lay claim to a higher class standing and to possession of the secret of the ages by their *ressentiment* listening or jazz cultism, or by making pretensions as culture consumers. Notice that in his typology of listener motives Adorno is able to present understandable relationships between various musical movements on the one hand and a given social structure on the other. His debunking approach undoubtedly has elicited resentment from some readers, but his commentaries are often both humorous and penetrating and can force one to see beyond one's own subjectivity.[24]

Of course, Adorno's typology does not exhaust the motivations that come into play in musical listening. Generally popular song music is listened to as entertainment, but other kinds of song may be selected for a variety of reasons. A particularly interesting example arose in the United States in the 1960s when political and life-style preferences influenced or were at least bound up with musical influences. There is a fairly long history behind the association of certain musical forms with various social and political stances. Folk music was for a long time a vehicle for radical working-class sentiments, for instance, and gatherings of old socialists to this day are the occasion for sing-alongs in which traditional picket line songs are sung for old time's sake. But the phenomenon of the 1960s was unique insofar as "radical" lyrics became the daily fare of the capitalist-owned mass media.

The Vietnam War created such a widespread emotional reaction that many usually apolitical people and apolitical aspects of life became politicized. In the pivotal year 1965, the song "Eve of Destruction" became a hit. Its antinuclear-war lyrics were the object of controversy, with political conservatives trying to ban it from the airwaves. A questionnaire survey of college students at San Francisco State University found, however, that only 14 percent of the respondents who had heard the song knew what the lyrics were really about. (Denisoff and Levine, 1971). Many more songs with antimilitary lyrics were to follow, but there is little evidence that the lyrics, as opposed to other expressions of antiwar feeling, persuaded many people.

Despite the fact that listeners did not seem to follow the meanings of song lyrics, certain musical activities such as attending rock concerts, purchasing records, and frequently listening to records correlated with college students having liberal or leftist political views as late as 1973. Radio listening, however, seemed to be correlated with political conservatism. Politically conservative students favored the current popular hits and "easy listening" music, while liberals tended to favor rock music, country-and-western music, or classical music, and favored even more pronouncedly jazz, folk music, blues, and protest music (Fox and Williams, 1974). By the 1970s the issues became more diffuse than the lingering Vietnam War. Mashkin and Volgy (1975), using a 1972 survey of some American college students, found that "political alienation" prevailed among those who preferred folk music, a middling level of political alienation obtained among the adherents of rock, and political conservatism characterized the country-and-western fans; moreover, "social alienation" (rejection of conventional institutions) was found among admirers of rock and folk music, while its absence characterized the followers of country-and-western. Rock and country-and-western enthusiasts favored traditional sex roles, while folk music enthusiasts did not. Country-and-western enthusiasts tended to be materialistic, while rock and folk enthusiasts did not. Only 10 percent of the sample, however, reported choosing their musical favorites on the basis of lyrics; an analysis of the remaining 90 percent, who did not choose their music according to the lyrics, yielded results which were identical to those given above for the whole population surveyed. Another study of American college students found that drug users listened more than others to the music of artists who lyrics included drug references, even though these listeners did not pay a great deal of attention to the lyrics (Bogg and Fair, 1974). In an analysis of the musical lyrics of the top hits and albums of the fall of 1974, Mashkin and Volgy found that any differences in sociopolitical content in the lyrics of the songs comprising the different styles had disappeared (Mashkin and Volgy, 1975: 456-457). Clearly the musical forms, not the lyrics, were emblems of different social and political mentalities.

The reasons why different social and political orientations correlate with given musical preferences are undoubtedly many. One possibility is that the social and political orientations are specific to one or two generations who also happen to share the same music; the correlation would thus be spurious, or accidental. Or a given medium, such as radio, may propagate a set of views indirectly through the subtle use of news and advertisements, and a given type of music may be broadcast most often in that medium. Again, the record companies and broadcast firms may use social and political symbolism to market their music; thus, even though listeners may not follow lyrics closely, they may comprehend the general thrust of them and accept or reject a musical style which is associated with the stance in question. In this last case, the music does not influence the listeners so much as it is packaged for them.

V. NONPROFESSIONAL PARTICIPATION

A significant factor in the characterization of musical roles is the incompatibility of the musical mentality with other concerns. The highly subjective nature of music does not allow for distractions from outside the subjective state, distractions which in objective thought are not distractions at all but "reality." The popular song writer was described as a role in which composition surrendered, as it were, to nonmusical concerns. Playing dance music seems to be the counterpart in the performance role. A parallel case in nonprofessional participation in social dancing. In a sensitive account of social dancing, Cottle (1966) reported distinct styles of sexual expression in dancing, role reciprocity patterns between and among dancing partners, shared meanings of dancing for different social and income ranks, etc.; but there evidently was nothing to report about any musical mentality. Indeed, some persons observed by Cottle demonstrated dance steps without the accompaniment of music at all, and a preference for such accompaniment seemed to be a matter of mere convention among upper-class people. Whether the current "disco" fashion of dancing entails any real involvement in music is yet to be investigated, but it is unlikely that there has been any real change since the "twist" era dancing studied by Cottle.

Dance is readily separable from music because it does not produce significant tones.[25] Perhaps a more ambiguous case occurs where the nonprofessional participant actually produces music but for nonmusical purposes. This is fairly common in societies where song is employed in courting rituals, as in the Ponapean and Trukese societies in the Caroline Islands. In Ponapean society there are both traditional love songs and newer ones; the latter have Western style melodies, use some non-Ponapean words, and tend to be shorter than the traditional songs. Young or middle-aged men sing them softly to the female who is the object of attention; third parties are not supposed to hear the song. Sometimes, however, the songs are sung in harmony by groups of drinking men, or loudly by little boys. Never are they sung by performers before an audience or at a feast. The songs have an aura of illegitimacy about them, since they are often used in adulterous affairs. Even among the unmarried they are associated with unapproved matches. Not surprisingly the lyrics are always ascribed to a male addressing a sweetheart. One of the unintentional side effects of the presence of Christian missionaries has been that sacrilegious references and sometimes hymn melodies are used. In Trukese society, where the males have a less secure social position, the lyrics are less aggressive and emphasize masochistic themes — e.g., psychological pain over a sweetheart's rejection (Fischer and Swartz, 1960). Although presumably one cannot make music without entering into a musical mentality, courting music would suggest coexistence of two mentalities at once, a feat of some complexity despite the taken-for-granted manner in which it occurs in the social world.

Moving from the abdication of the musical mentality, which seems to typify dancing, and maintaining simultaneous mentalities, which seems to typify courting ritual music, and moving toward conditions in which the musical mentality seems to dominate, there is the case of work music. In work music, the participant is involved in a physical task which is intrinsically uninteresting. Abhoring a mental vacuum, workers use song as a mechanism of self-preoccupation or even of group preoccupation. In a study of early twentieth-century black American work songs, Odum and Johnson (1964: 149) found three kinds of work songs: those originating in the culture industry or some other external source, variations and improvisations upon borrowed material, and true folk songs originating in the underclass. The variations upon borrowed material and the true folk songs reflect typical conversations which might occur in the daily situations of life. Odum and Johnson give one example in which the western ballad "Casey Jones" is transformed in part into instructions from Casey Jones to his fireman (1964: 150). The work song may reflect the social world in which it is found when it occasions such innovations.

Somewhat different from social dancing, courting songs, and work songs is the involvement of nonprofessionals in completely musical occasions. Small groups may play chamber music in the home, sing around a piano, play guitars in a favorite hangout, participate in a barbershop quartet, or play an instrument when alone. In these situations music is the reason for the individual or group's activity, and it receives more or less undivided attention. The musical focus may be the object for which people gather together, or it may spontaneously emerge around a camp fire on a beach or in a hotel room during a convention.

Among bluegrass enthusiasts the jam session, named after the jazz performer's practice, has evolved as a quasi institution.[26] Although frequently described as authentic American folk music, bluegrass is a genre of commercial popular music that originated after World War II. It gained popularity outside the country music audience in the late 1950s and early '60s during the urban "folk music" revival. The first bluegrass festivals were held in the late 1960s, and the number has increased since then. The festivals last two or three days and are held annually throughout the United States in large, open rustic areas. While there are formal performances by professional groups on stages, a major attraction for many attending the festivals is the opportunity to participate in "shadetree" or "parking lot pickin." These informal musical groupings are a distinctive aspect of bluegrass festivals; a large percentage of the audiences can and do play instruments during the course of the activities. In fact, it is common for the professional performers to join the jam sessions after they have concluded their stage appearances.

Bluegrass style usually entails a melody sung in a high tenor with harmony parts both above and below the melody line. Instrumentation often includes guitar and bass fiddle for accompaniment and solo roles for fiddle, banjo, and mandolin. The bluegrass blend of shaped note (Sacred Harp), blues (flattened fifths and sevenths), and mountain string band traditions requires instrumental virtuosity in fast tempos and syncopated rhythms. Typically, a vocal rendition is alternated with choruses of three- or four-part harmony and instrumental interludes. Nostalgic lyrics predominate. Electric instruments are prohibited and sometimes also intoxicants. Dancing is discouraged and where present, is segregated from other activities.

While friends and acquaintances may engage in a jam session, sessions frequently take place among relative strangers. Ritually they begin with conversation, proceed with a suggestion to play a little, which is followed by mild protests of limited ability, followed by actual performance. While one performer is assuming a solo role, it is incumbent upon the others to provide a nondisruptive accompaniment. Furthermore, each participant capable of taking a solo break is expected to do so, and it is expected that breaks will not be dominated by any single individual without the implicit agreement of others. Leadership in a jam session is allocated according to evidenced musical ability. The leader suggests songs, plays solo parts, and assigns parts for others. The allocation of parts is done by means of eye contact, and reciprocating eye contact becomes the mechanism through which status is negotiated. Offenders against the normative structure are excluded by the suggestion of songs they do not know or by pushing the individual beyond his or her abilities in order to create embarrassment. If these devices do not work, the musicians will abandon the session rather than create a confrontation. The enforcement of norms must be distinguished from a competitive situation, which occurs when instrumentalists with identical instruments join a session. The competitors alternately display virtuosity until one recognizes the other as superior and plays a subordinate role.

3
Social Organization and Music

I. MUSICAL INSTITUTIONALIZATION

As described in earlier chapters, music appears to be a rather fragile phenomenon. It depends upon someone's attention in order to so much as exist; someone must follow the sounds as if listening to a conversation initiated by the performer. If the temporal relationships of the music were lost by a lapse in the subject-object tension, by a disruption of the mentality, the music would be lost. Hence, there is an insecurity about music, a reason to fear that it might be lost or insufficiently propagated. The survivability of any given musical meaning simply does not inspire confidence.

In the phraseology of I. C. Jarvie, music is "mind-dependent." It is not alone in its fragility, because every cultural artifact is mind-dependent. When some level of continuity emerges in history, something has happened in human interaction where a complex of actions has become a routine. By refusing to honor routine-based meanings, such as the value of money, one may make all that is stable wobble a bit, but as a rule most recognized routines and the meanings that go with them have the force of inertia on their side. They are institutions (Jarvie, 1972: 147).

The motivating force behind musical institutions should be immediately apparent. Music is transitory; hence people attempt to give it some permanence in institutions. Strictly speaking, the attempt is doomed to failure because transitory experiences cannot be frozen in perpetuity without becoming something other than the experiences which are valued and desired. Nevertheless, the coherence of musical traditions depends upon musical institutions, and without some coherent base the tones would be perceived as mere noise. Thus the apparent incompatibility between musicality and institutionality is in reality a dialectical relationship. This, of course, does not prevent one winning out over the other, thus undermining both.

Institutions are not generally dreamed up anew; they succeed more readily when there is a pre-existing familiarity with what

74

would be institutionalized. The process of institutionalization may be preceded by habitualization. An individual's personal habits make life easier by supplanting a myriad of trivial decisions with formulae. The formulae are adopted without a great deal of personal consideration because they already have a history of practical success behind them. In the case of institutionalization, a plurality of people reciprocally recognize a habitual mode of conduct by which they influence one another. There is a mutual orientation arising from interaction, and the routine actions associated with that mutual orientation are understood to be typical lines of activity (see Berger and Luckmann, 1967: 54). Familiar examples range from the institution of marriage, to certain conventions of conversation, dietary customs, and the like.

In an early study Max Kaplan (1944) conducted a survey of the musical institutions of a small city, Pueblo, Colorado.[1] The discussion was devoted to the agencies of musical education (schools, private teachers, tutorial bands), the media of music circulation (radio, libraries, music stores, the musicians' union), music production organizations (orchestras, private groups, ethnic organizations) and music consumption institutions (clubs, churches, dance halls, jukeboxes, etc.). A community study of that kind can serve as a useful model for applied research in other communities. In the present context, however, it illustrates the variety of musical institutions.

The word *music* today carries with it the connotation of a fully mature and independent art, but it took centuries of institutionalization for this development to take place. Symphonies, chamber music, and solo instrumental compositions especially are relatively modern forms. In ancient Greece, music in its broadest sense meant any of the arts and sciences that came under the patronage of the mythical muses, those imaginary maidens who were the daughters of Zeus and Mnemosyne, the goddess of memory. This was a fanciful way of indicating that music was recorded inspiration. It included lyric poetry, tragic and comic drama, choral dancing, and song, as well as astronomy and history. Thus music corresponded to our liberal arts or high culture.

The fact that for the Greeks music was not a separate art gave music an importance quite different from its modern significance. The Greeks had noted that scale intervals could be coordinated with mathematical ratios. The discovery, attributed to Pythagoras, showed that intervals such as the octave, fifth, and fourth had a mathematical relationship. When a tuned string is stopped off exactly in the middle, the musical interval between the unstopped string and the divided one is the octave, and the mathematical ratio is 1:2. If a segment of the string divided into halves is compared with a segment of a string divided into three parts, the interval will be the fifth, and the ratio 2:3, etc. To Pythagoras and his followers music thus reflected order and proportion and rested on a demonstrably rational basis. It suggested that the rest of the universe could be reduced to numerical relationships. This idea found its way into other aspects of Greek thought, which sought for a cosmic harmony. That music is thought of so differently today, despite technical advances in rationalizing it, shows how much it has been institutionalized as a performance specialty.

Guilds and Unions

Professional musicians — that is, those who make their living by music — have often had to create formal organizations for their own economic protection. In the late medieval and early Renaissance era in northern Europe, musicians' associations emerged both in towns and in wider regions. These guilds sought to establish monopolies for the benefit of their members and against the seemingly unfair competition of amateurs. The financial backing of the nobility and municipal legal cooperation needed to maintain such monopolies was not always forthcoming. Guild organization in France began in Paris in the fourteenth century and expanded through a centralized organization into other cities. Late seventeenth-century litigation eventually broke the monopoly, which had become somewhat meaningless anyway after the crown sold the monopoly guarantees at public auction. In England associations were formed at the county level, in the city of London, and in the royal court. Puritan opposition to musical entertainment resulted in a weakening of the economic status of musicians, and the restored crown was not particularly reliable in bettering conditions (Loft, 1950: 72-99, 118-161, 212-271). Thus government sponsored monopolies did not seem to be a very successful strategem for the musical profession.

Musicians' trade unions began in Europe in the second half of the nineteenth century, when the individual musician was in an entirely unfavorable bargaining position with organizers, opera impressarios, and theater managers. The unions replaced benefit societies. Similar unions were formed in the United States and

South America in the late 1800s (Loft, 1950: 276-388). The unionizing of major American symphony orchestras and opera orchestras occasioned some prolonged conflicts, which affected the history of studio music as well. Today the musician has access to detailed information and guidelines related to salary, modes of payment, and legal aspects of the profession, all made available through the union. Individual negotiations are still common, but they are most often based on levels of compensation above the minimum union scale, especially in cases where performers play particularly important instruments or hold principal positions (see Bensman, 1967: 56).

While the economic concerns of guilds and unions may seem inconsistent with artistic concerns, they are by no means irrelevant. Artistic excellence usually requires an investment of time and resources which is sufficiently great as to exclude other economic pursuits. Professional status made possible by economic organization thus makes artistic sense. In defending their economic positions, musicians have also defended music.

Performance Organizations

The econocentrism of the musicians' guilds and unions is matched by that of orchestra and opera company managements. The magnitude of the task of organizing, funding, and staging a serious music production with an orchestra or an opera company requires a centralized bureaucracy. In the commercial world, a monopoly or near monopoly could meet such financial burdens. Music organizations usually prefer to seek the suport of a foundation. The situation is different with popular music, where audience-oriented, simplified styles requiring only small ensembles allow small firms to compete. While artistic concerns often come into conflict with bureaucratic thinking and practical exigencies such as production costs in much serious music, they may be altogether abandoned in the rush to secure brand names (stars) and uncomplicated rhythmic structures in the case of popular music (Kaplan, 1951: 59-61).

The extramusical entities of organizations and markets, though creations of humans, end up controlling people. This control creates a world of ironies and injustices manifesting the fundamental dilemma of institutionalization. A case in point was the popularization of black music in the United States. Because of the segregation of entertainment establishments, blacks were not able to present their music in lucrative settings. For example, Paul Whiteman — however well-intentioned — made a fortune by appropriating black music (jazz), having it arranged in classical Western harmony, and playing it in upper-class establishments. Meanwhile, black jazz bands were limited to lower-class, segregated establishments and even to ghetto record labels; the black performers lived in relative poverty, though their music was being distributed in impure form to the upper classes (Rieger and Rublein, 1974).

Even serious music is greatly influenced by market pressures. The German operatic tradition, for example, grew in a number of large and medium-sized provincial theaters. These developed a stable ensemble of vocalists who were used to working together. In the twentieth century, however, the market demands international names. Thus musical virtuosi are flown in to meet with a star conductor, who must somehow shape a coherent performance incorporating the roving stars and a local supporting cast. Clearly the smaller of the traditional companies are left in a difficult situation by this state of affairs (Adorno, 1976: 78).

In the United States box office demands often determine opera repertory. The staging of opera is enormously expensive, and any production which may draw only a limited audience is simply an imprudent venture (Martorella, 1977). Even more limiting are the cost increases occasioned by new works. Company managers must take into account the fact that an unfamiliar work will require extra rehearsal time. Sometimes it is simply a matter of the size of the cast and extras. For instance in the early 1970s *Aïda* filled the Metropolitan Opera to 98 percent capacity and still lost $29,000.00 per performance, while *Madam Butterfly* only filled the hall to 94 percent capacity but lost only $13,000.00 per performance (Martorella, 1974: 154–166).[2] Life for the big companies is complicated by the star system also. Even the best vocalists are vulnerable to attacks of flu as well as other emergencies; so every contract for a star must be coupled with an arrangement for a near-star to serve as a last minute substitute. The near-star agrees to serve as a "cover" on the condition that a performance of the role is scheduled for him or her as well. Then, of course, it is necessary to find someone willing to cover for the near-star on those dates. These intricate arrangements must be reconciled with both audience demands and artistic imperatives (Martorella, 1974: 174–238, 247ff.).

The principal art music function in Europe has been the

opera; in the United States it has been the symphony orchestra concert. While at first conductors had to educate American audiences away from vocal music and are still educating them away from solo instrumental virtuosi, it is still expected that a symphony or symphonic poem will serve as the center piece of a concert. Hence, European conductors who were primarily opera conductors have come to the United States to specialize in orchestral works. After some experiments in commercial, co-operative, and even demagogic models of organization, the American symphony orchestra has evolved a philanthropically supported form of organization which is subject to the interests of its patrons as well as simple box-office appeal (Mueller, 1951: 22-35).

The British and American experiences illustrate two different models of symphony orchestra organization. Both the Philharmonic Society of London and the New York Philharmonic Orchestra began as musicians' co-operatives, whose membership included a large segment of German musicians. The London organization began as a sideline of music teachers, who took turns at service as conductors and soloists. Since they wished to differentiate themselves and their audiences from the working class, they insisted that subscribers to the season had to be approved by the society. Eventually, under financial pressure, the organization shifted to public admission, used the star system, and exploited its snob appeal to bolster audiences. Occasional economic depressions and the disruption effected by World War I brought the society to difficult financial straits; Sir Thomas Beecham, a conductor and wealthy gentleman, rescued the Philharmonic Society in exchange for his one-man control of the organization. However, Beecham was not able to offer the members full-time employment, and in 1918 the Philharmonic Society returned to its co-operative form of organization. Meanwhile competition appeared when the BBC Orchestra was organized, and Beecham established the London Philharmonic Orchestra. Under this pressure, the Philharmonic Society of London finally hired the London Philharmonic Orchestra for its season and simply served as a sponsor for that orchestra. With the onset of World War II, this system too collapsed, and the Philharmonic Society again returned to co-operative arrangement (1939), with the Society sponsoring its own orchestra and playing for other sponsors as well. This mode of operation in effect copied that of the London Symphony Orchestra (established 1904). The British government provided support after the war, obviating the need for private patrons. Although there are five orchestras in London, the co-operative mode of organization seems to be surviving even amid the competition (Couch, 1976).

The early New York Philharmonic was also a co-operative in the nineteenth century, but it was more explicitly intended as a means of providing employment opportunity for musicians. It accumulated debts during several economic depressions, but a model solution seemed to be in view when Henry Lee Higginson rescued the similarly troubled Boston Symphony Orchestra in 1881, assuming the BSO's debts and placing the performers on a concert system. The New York Symphony was organized on the Boston model, and by 1911 the New York Philharmonic had found a board of wealthy patrons and adopted a contract system in order to compete with the Symphony; thus, its members became full-time employees rather than part-time free-lancers, an arrangement having obvious artistic advantages. The Philharmonic and Symphony eventually merged to form the modern organization (Couch, 1976; Mueller, 1951). This philanthropic foundation form of organization has provided stability and an authority structure capable of making difficult artistic decisions, but it has proved to be no more immune to financial pressures than the co-operative model. The American symphony orchestras have come to be increasingly dependent on governmental support, as have other philanthropically supported artistic institutions. The Philadelphia Orchestra, the most financially secure orchestra in the United States, receives 66 percent of its income from earnings — mostly box-office returns. Twenty-seven percent comes from nongovernmental unearned sources, and 7 percent from public funds. Other orchestras rely more on public sources, both under the form of out-and-out unearned support and contracts to present performances in schools and parks (Netzer, 1978: 113–117).

Religion and Music

In some respects religion and music are alike. Both entail a mode of consciousness which is not encompassed within the boundaries of objective experience. In fact, the empirical data (sounds) remain just at the level of a stepping-stone pointing to the direction that consciousness can go. As in religion, where an idea or experience such as prayer is a direction rather than an experience of the divine, in music a mode of consciousness can be reached that cannot be judged simply through empirical methods.

Music and religion seem to occur in the same kind of experiential region, but the sharing of that area has not been altogether peaceful. The early Christian church opposed professional music altogether, citing its association with immoral theater, pagan ritual, and state militarism. Musicians had to abandon their work to convert to Christianity. However, after Constantine's edict in 313 making Christianity the state religion, vocal music was gradually incorporated into worship — creating a tension between sacred and secular music. Church musicians were not to become virtuosi but liturgical leaders and teachers; instrumental music was banned from the churches (Loft, 1950: 17-22). Since many musicians were slaves in the Roman Empire, and since many female slaves could only be freed by converting to Christianity, the route to freedom, for female musicians was often a religious one, which entailed abandoning their musical involvement. Later in Christianity a far more intellectual approach was used in setting religious policy toward musicians; the influential theologian Thomas Aquinas distinguished between the music profession itself, which he took to be acceptable, and the improper uses to which it might be put (Loft, 1950: 22-35). Of course, the Christian churches had used music as an ally since late Roman times, to break the spell of the objective mentality and to induce the onset of worship mentalities. Islam both rewarded and persecuted musicians because Mohammed himself sometimes favored music, giving it status in heaven, and at other times prohibited it. Moslem theologians have been divided over the propriety of music from early on (Loft, 1950: 22-23). Recently, the Iranian religious leader, Khomeini, has been persecuting popular music. In general, then, it can be said that organized religion has sometimes hindered musical institutionalization and at other times been its agent.

Much of the institutionalization of Western music can be traced to Western monasticism. Odo, abbot of Cluny from 927 to 942, is known to have arranged the tones of the scale into an orderly progression from A to G and to have established pitches and intervals. This enabled choirs to learn works from notation rather than having to learn by rote in the Schola Cantorum that Pope Gregory the Great had established in Rome. In the eleventh century, another monk, Guido of Arezzo, added the lined staff to Odo's notation, and used a hymn to St. John as a pedagogical device to associate certain sounds with notes — leading to the modern do re mi system. In their treatises, Odo and Guido approached music as a means for singing praise to the Creator, and they dismissed the Greek-inspired speculation that music held a key to the universe. During the ninth, tenth, and eleventh centuries, monastic music also saw the beginnings of polyphony, with its attendant specializations within musical performance.

One of the less fortunate aspects of both religion and music is their susceptibility for use by cultural and social elites to divert the attention of the lower classes from the practical task of creating a more just social order. Since the 1960s, when religion became part of a worldwide social movement to raise social consciousness and to remove class and racial barriers to human and economic rights, it has become increasingly difficult to point to cases of religion serving as a social distraction, much less becoming allied with music in such a process. In some backwaters, however, the phenomenon still occurs. Souffrant (1970) has found this kind of occurrence in his analysis of a children's hymnal published in 1954 and still in use decades later in Haiti.[3]

An interesting analysis of the way music and religion help institutionalize one another in a common mentality was made by a sociologist who participated for some years in a Hindu church in California. Joseph Damrell was given the cymbal-playing role by the swami. The cymbals were small bells used in the vespers worship to keep a steady rhythm throughout a hymn on the first, fifth, and seventh beats of a slow, ten-beat cycle. The vocal music moves in waves and

> After many practice sessions and numerous attempts on my part to occasion some sort of recognition of the fundamentals of music performance, I have come to the conclusion that the event is so much a personal act of worship for the participants that any sort of collective effort is impossible. . . .
>
> For a couple of years, the Swami's comments after Vespers would include mention of how my cymbal-playing fared. Occasionally he would call my playing a "massacre." (Damrell, 1977: 157–158)

The "massacre" seemed to be an irregularity in the beat that would cause a snap in the meditative attention to the supra-objective. Religious consciousness, as opposed to mundane consciousness, would be lost in such a massacre.

Most people have some familiarity with the use of hymns in worship. At set times the congregation, sometimes led by a specialist and sometimes accompanied by an organ or piano, sings several verses of a song which has religiously inspired lyrics. Other kinds of music are also used in worship services. A solo organist may set the mood before the formal service begins, fill in gaps during the proceedings with mellow interludes, or conclude the service with a rousing recessional. A choir may in effect give a performance as part of the services, or a clergyman in a liturgically oriented religion may sing some of the important texts of the occasion. Guitars, flutes, violins, and other instruments may be used. Various prayers may be sung by a choir or by a congregation to simple melodies with notes of varying value enabling the musical text to be adjusted to the verbal text. In Christian monasticism, such devices are used several times a day to sing the biblical psalms.

In contrast to such scheduled, more or less fixed liturgical uses, there are more spontaneous uses of music in religion. In the Apostolic Church of John Maranke, for example, a body in Central Africa, the congregations recognize and use two different kinds of worship music. One kind consists of planned hymns, scheduled by the church officials. The other kind is initiated from the congregation to bring a speaker's message to a climax (or end). This second kind is entirely negotiable; someone begins singing from a seated position and, if joined by others, gets up, walks around, and encourages the congregation to sing. If the speaker wishes to continue, the song initiator may cease, but the action of the congregation determines the outcome. Or the speaker may vigorously join in the song, bring it to a conclusion, and then continue speaking (Jules-Rosette, 1975). In such a setting, music is clearly an adjunct of religious enthusiasm, and it may or may not be attributed to some supernatural entity's influence.

Commercial Music Distribution

While the population is made up of vastly different kinds of people with equally vast differences in musical taste, the distribution system manages to touch nearly all of these people and often even brings them the music they want to hear. Few people are naive enough to believe that the invisible hand of the "market system" matches the consumer's musical needs with the right product; a good part of the market is sold on a work before the work is sold to it. The remarkable aspect of the music distribution system is thus the thorough sales job it manages. Horkheimer and Adorno (1972: 123) speak of the "ruthless unity in the culture industry" wherein "something is provided for all so that none may escape." Just as propaganda artists pitch the same basic line to different audiences, so the culture industry's strategems bring the basic message — that the consumer must accept what industry provides — through various stylistic alternatives.

When radio was a major medium for adult Americans, the major radio networks functioned in a manner similar to the major television networks of today. Programming was aimed at the bulk of the population which had money to spend. It may be that the networks had not found the lowest common denominator in the heyday of radio, as they seem to have found for the television audiences today, but they aimed at the general adult public and carried a good deal of advertising traffic. With the advent of television, radio lost much of its advertising market. Nevertheless, the development of cheap transistor models expanded radio's potential, and many small broadcasting firms entered the business without any network affiliation supplying programming. The void was filled by playing records over the air, since they were the cheapest program material available (Hirsch, 1969).

Studies showed that it was teenagers who were listening to the new stations on transistor radios; the targets for the "top forty" music were therefore teenagers, with smaller markets being met by other radio stations. Teenagers generally have the resources for small purchases such as records, and thus the substance of the programming became as much a commercial as the advertisements. The distribution system which evolved has been sufficiently successful that no great alterations were made to adjust to the shrinkage of the youth market in the 1970s (see Rieger, 1974).

Radio is by far the largest distribution influence available to the culture industry; a 1955 study showed that it reached 86 percent of college student respondents. Hearing others play music in informal settings ranked second at 69 percent; listening to records was third at 66 percent; listening to television fourth at 65 percent; and public concerts ranked fifth at 62 percent.[4] Obviously a taste for classical music is not propagated in the distribution system, artistic taste seems to stem from the influence of relatives, attending live performances of serious music, and studying an instrument (Fathi and Heath, 1974, in a study of male university students in western Canada). Indeed, in many localities serious music can be found only on public-supported radio stations; some places do not even have that. Radio audience studies show that in fact the broadcasters succeed in selling their product to the intended audiences. "Top forty" music appeals to the youngest groups, "up-tempo middle of the road" (U-MOR) and "beautiful" music appeals to those over thirty-six. All categories of music broadcast have some following in the listening public (Peterson and Davis, 1974). The "sale" of broadcasts closely parallels the sale of records (see Levine and Denisoff, 1972).

The radio public seems ready to lap up everything promoted to it; the policy of some stations of playing records for a fee paid by the record companies rather than relying on the choices of disc jockeys does not affect audience ratings (Etzkorn, 1959: 150–151). Nevertheless, market response becomes such an overriding concern that popular music performers will only perform works which industry representatives say will be plugged. Today music publishers in effect serve as songwriters' agents because of their connections and prestige in the record industry.[5] The performer's name recognition, a factor which influences radio acceptance and record sales, is an important factor; indeed, the main difference between a songwriter's demonstration record and a commercially produced record is that the latter is recorded with union musicians and one or more name performers. The whole process is built on guesswork as to what will make a "hit" (Etzkorn, 1959: 156–188).

The cost of producing, packaging, and promoting records is high. At least 75,000 to 80,000 albums must be sold before the break-even point is reached. Seventy-four percent of singles and 61 percent of pop albums do not return their initial investment. Only the larger recording companies have enough superstars to survive the decline of any one of them; small companies rise or fall with the fortunes of one or two acts (Denisoff and Levine, 1972). Despite the fact that many companies fold, the record industry has become less centralized than it once was. Before 1956 four firms almost completely dominated the field because they could promote their products through broadcast networks and theaters. RCA Victor was corporately linked with NBC and with RKO Films, which had a network of theaters. Columbia was linked with CBS; Decca with Music Corporation of America and Universal Studios, which held a theater chain; and Capitol was linked to Paramount Pictures and its theaters until 1950. Then the United States Supreme Court in an antitrust decision forced the movie companies to sell their theater chains, thereby weakening the control of eight companies over the motion picture industry. Secondary effects of the decision were that the "big four" record labels lost their automatic distribution through theater chains and that several movie companies needed to invest the cash proceeds from the sale of their theaters. MGM, United Artists, Paramount, Warner Brothers, and Twentieth Century Fox then went into the record business. At the same time decentralization in the radio broadcast industry expanded the channels through which records might be given public exposure. Thus from 1957 to 1969 as the record industry became decentralized, frantic competition ensued (Peterson and Berger, 1975).

The key role in a record company is that of the producer; a large firm will have a number of them, each responsible for six or more acts or name performers. The producer maintains contact with the performers, faithfully makes the rounds of nightspots to keep up on entertainment trends, personalities, and songs, and sorts out the various demonstration tapes sent or brought in. The producer sets repertory, making the name performer believe the choices represent a mutual decision. The role also entails organizing recording sessions, calculating the enormous costs of performers' and engineers' time, and negotiating the packaging and plugging format with the promotion department. Control over producers is accomplished in classic bureaucratic fashion; record company executives must approve all budget decisions. Approval for speculative ventures is usually contingent upon a recent history of market success (Peterson and Berger, 1971).

Two sets of people serve as gatekeepers in the commercial music world. One consists of radio station program directors, who select two to four new records per week for broadcast from the 150 to 200 records produced each week. The other set consists of the record reviewers who write for such periodicals as *Rolling Stone, Creem, Phonograph Record Magazine,* and others and consequently are bombarded with samples and promotional material (Denisoff and Levine, 1972). The ultimate criterion, the last gatekeeper, of course, is the buying public. The popularity charts created by the trade weeklies, *Billboard, Cashbox,* and *Record World* reflect where the public's money is being spent. The charts assess radio exposure time and record sales in the twenty-two most populated American regional markets. Within each market area the radio stations with the largest listenership within each category of popular music are monitored, as well as the major retail record sales outlets in each area. The trade weeklies send rating forms to managers of radio stations and sales outlets to be filled out and returned. The retail sales form asks the respondent to select and rank the top sellers, out of a list of some two hundred singles, and to evaluate all two hundred on a scale of sales action. The station form asks for the radio station "playlist" of twenty-five to forty ranked recordings, with a 1 to 8 "pick list" chosen from recent new releases. The stations vary in their methods of constructing their "playlists," but they usually use local market studies, local requests, and reviews in the trade periodicals. The data are weighed by the trade weeklies and then edited according to subjectively inspired criteria to produce the charts (Hesbacker, Downing, and Berger, 1975).

The interesting thing about this market response system is that the public has little control over the content of the music. Record producers select songs and artists which will succeed in appearing high in the charts; pluggers tell station managers and retail managers what will succeed; finally the charts measure the success which the pre-selected material has enjoyed. In short, the companies talk to themselves through this complex system. The public dutifully follows what has been promoted. Thus the charts measure the success of a sales campaign rather than shifts in musical taste. Indeed, the music seems almost beside the point in this process, while the industry is busy convincing itself of its sales prowess.[6]

An intriguing aspect of this commercial kind of institutionalization of popular music is what Bennett (1979) called secondary popular culture. Many local performing groups imitate the commercial recordings, and their success depends upon the faithfulness of their imitation (see Blaukopf, 1974: 18–19). Why, asks Bennett, do people pay the imitators when they can hear the original on records? It must be that the live, imitative performances mark a social order different from that of the private home where the records may be played, and different even from that of "disco" establishments. Thus, the actual music, while supporting a complete social form in the case of radio and phonographic music, is only one element in a different pop music social form, the live performance. The latter seems to require the stage phenomenon, with the visible presence of the performers. The performers' gyrations, and even mechanical movements of the stage itself, accompanied by strobe lights and other props, have become essential to the secondary popular music institutionalization.

This secondary popular culture of the mid-to-late twentieth century seems to parallel a much older phenomenon. In England in the late nineteenth and early twentieth centuries, when music distribution was accomplished through the sale of sheet music on a large scale, the publishers organized ballad concerts to plug their products. Star vocalists and composers drew audiences, who then purchased the sheet music for what they had heard. While the music included occasional opera arias, most of the material was of a sentimental, undemanding nature equivalent to today's top forty. The middle class, unable to afford professional musicians for home entertainment, used the sheet music when entertaining their guests, and the guests were expected to be ready to reciprocate in kind. This practice required that one attend ballad concerts and read news reports about the concerts in order to know what was deemed current and tasteful — neither art music, which was too serious, nor music that was considered too common (Pearsall, 1975: 74ff., 119ff.). Thus, a secondary popular music imitated the professional performers' popular music.

II. MUSIC AND SOCIAL INEQUALITY

In all communities and organizations, some people have more power, prestige, or property than others. In whole societies, some groups collectively comprise a class or stratum with certain privileges, or they are merely the beneficiaries of favorable treatment from others even when there is no formal right or privilege involved. However, the ranking of persons is only the most obvious aspect of this "stratification," as sociologists call it. The ranking of persons is as obvious to the untrained observer as it is to the questionnaire technician who measures rankings with scales of reputation, income, and education.

Take, for example, a very commonplace occurrence, at least commonplace for sociology professors. A stranger begins to strike up a conversation with small talk, perhaps in a waiting room or on an airplane. The small talk touches upon some social issue about which the sociologist has some organized thought and precise conceptualizations. It does not take long for the stranger to structure the small talk differently out of a sense of ranking — either avoiding topics which would put himself or herself at a conversational disadvantage or entering with greater interest in an exchange which might have begun as a simple commentary on the weather. The stranger, whether finding the exchange agreeable or disagreeable, can most likely place the sociologist on a social standing scale without measuring income, occupational ranking, or years of formal education.

Not only in conversations, but also in mannerisms, the organization of one's life, appearance of residence and the like, social standings in a system of inequality are conveyed to people with a high degree of precision. It is not a matter of obvious symbols of high status. When some people live in an upper-class neighborhood they are looked down upon and when they drive expensive cars they are deemed vulgar. Similarly when some people live below their means they are not fooling anybody. Some exude class no matter how modest their income and others fail to make convincing presentations of class no matter how secure they are. There are thousands of little cues that people assess with a great deal of subtlety. Forcing a display of a few cues that one might have some control over accomplishes nothing if a thousand others contradict it; in fact, it may be counter-productive if one seems to be faking.

Musical conduct enters the world of social inequality in the same way as all other conduct. It conveys standing to others and to oneself, and its instances of faking a particular status are as easily picked up as other cases of unconvincing presentations of self. People will embody their status genuinely or emit mixed messages through music as well as through every other aspect of their lives. It must be recalled, however, that social status and musical sophistication are not the same. Sometimes high status and musical simplicity have been associated — for example, in the Soviet policy preferring light classical to contemporary innovative styles.

Sometimes the very instrument played has class implications. The lute was "courtly" in England in Elizabethan times; this had obvious implications for the kind of solo music composed and the financial security of lute soloists. When the piano gained popularity in middle-class life, the organ remained associated with church and court, simply because of the relative expense of the two instruments; thus piano music evolved as middle-class music to be marketed in the new industrial world (see Weber, 1958: 111, 120–124). With the rise of the music market, composers could become entrepreneurs rather than servants, although business conditions affected them variously. Rossini, for instance, became well-to-do with the backing of the Rothschilds, while Wagner never received much for his early works though they filled theaters. Brahms, Verdi, Richard Strauss, and Puccini received full returns on their investments of labor (Adorno, 1976: 55ff.).

Sometimes the musical content of compositions can be further understood as expressions of particular classes in particular historical settings. Beethoven's music in part reflects the early nineteenth-century demands of the evolving middle class for reason and freedom; the musical form is highly rationalized and yet it broke from traditional patterns. It is said, for instance, that Wagner's music reflects the situation of the middle class in Germany, powerless without the emergence of a truly capitalist society, his music emphasizes pervasive force over the rationalized forms inherited from Beethoven (Adorno, 1976: 62-63). Of course, all such interpretation requires previous knowledge of class situations and typical mentalities. One cannot learn a great deal about nineteenth-century Europeans by analyzing their music alone.

The fact that the twentieth-century distribution system purveys music as a market item, often with no respect for artistic quality, naturally has consequences in regard to the class system. Those who stand outside the market, either as an elite looking down upon it or as an economically marginal group which it does not cater to, may escape the hold of market music. Serious music composers and aspiring composition students have been shown to have upper- and middle-class backgrounds, for instance (Nash, 1957) — i.e., they do not often come from the ranks of the mass market. They have also been shown to have more general education than popular songwriters (Etzkorn, 1959: 294). Among music students in New York City, the upper classes tended to study at the Julliard School and focus on piano, while the lower classes tended to study at the Manhattan School and focus on theory, an education career track (Kadushin, 1969: 392). Thus the class system is observable in musical roles even though musicians as a rule do not overtly identify with any particular class position (see Kaplan, 1951: 235).

One of the earliest listenership surveys, done in Evansville, Indiana, showed that classical and light classical music had the greatest appeal for the upper classes, while jazz and hillbilly music had the greatest appeal for the lower classes (Schuessler, 1948). Two decades later a quite different situation existed among a Los Angeles student population, where classical music appealed most to the lower class (those whose fathers had unskilled occupations) as well as the upper class (those whose fathers were professionals) (Denisoff and Levine, 1972: 248). The implications however are the same in both cases. Non-mass-market music appealed to the fringes of the population rather than to those in the mass consumer strata which are the object of large-scale marketing techniques and strategems.

An interesting case of class dynamics in music is the popularization of black music in the United States. Black slaves and post-

Civil-War agricultural workers developed both work songs and stage performances for whites' social events. White entertainers began to imitate this underclass tradition in a minstrel genre of music, which was a rough stereotype of black music. Some blacks later imitated the imitation. Meanwhile, jazz developed among blacks with the incorporation of European musical instruments into their music. Ragtime was a syncretism of black rhythms and European music, while blues represented an adaptation of the harmonies of American black music. Eventually, jazz developed into a multifaceted spectrum with the improvisation-centered jam session at one end and the big band symphonic jazz at the other (Slotkin, 1943). Musical influences crossed the barriers of inequality, though not without difficulty. The expressiveness of the black tradition conflicted with middle-class reserve (Kaplan, 1951: 54). Leaders of the white communities, especially educators and persons concerned with "public morality," opposed the acceptance of jazz. They identified it with crime, vice, and sexual license, evidently basing such judgments on their stereotypes of the American black. Opposition to jazz was particularly strong in the South, where the blacks' social position was lower than elsewhere in the country (Berger, 1947).

For those living in a class society, it is difficult to comprehend how virtually every aspect of life becomes an opportunity to express inequality. In music, what is most trivial may embody a massive social tendency. In a 1971 study of English adolescents, Murdock and McCron found that pop music did not unite them into a common, age-specific subculture, but rather that different kinds of pop musical records separated the middle-class adolescents from the working-class adolescents. Moreover, interviews revealed that the adolescents themselves associated "scoobies" (college-bound middle-class youth) and "skins" (school dropouts from the working-class) with different kinds of pop music. Class hostilities crossed over into the musical world as well.

> Although pop has undoubtedly extended the range of expressive styles open to adolescents, we would argue that their underlying values and definitions continue to come from class-based systems, rather than from pop. Our findings so far suggest that rather than creating a classless society of the young, pop is reaffirming class divisions. (Murdock and McCron, 1973: 692)

A similar phenomenon arose in Brazil some years earlier. The traditional music of the lower-class, black population had a steady tempo; white middle-class youth in the Brazilian cities, taking a cue from the discontinuous rhythmic accentuations in postwar dance music, reacted against the traditional rhythm. The appearance of the "Bossa Nova" style in Rio de Janeiro marked the definitive withdrawal from the samba and its folk sources. The samba, which preserved a basic correspondence between percussion and suitable neuromuscular response, had experienced change largely in melodies. After 1950, however, the social classes physically separated from one another in Rio de Janeiro, with the poor living in the hills in the north of the city and the comfortable living in the south. Youth of the comfortable class were completely separated from folk musical tradition as a result; they no longer participated in the lower-class culture as their predecessors had. By 1958, an entirely untraditional style, played by a group of lads between seventeen and twenty-two years old, became popular (Ramos, 1974: 221-222). Thus the class divisions were by then fully reflected in Brazilian popular music. In the 1960s the popular music composers of the country attempted to identify with the poor by idealizing traditional music, but soon protest songs against the military regime emerged. The latter songs suggest a cosmopolitanism in which traditional strains may be blended but which nevertheless goes well beyond the lower-class traditions.

One example of the effect inequality can have on music is the "folk music" phenomenon. A folk song is a traditional song preserved in a noncosmopolitan culture. Since cosmopolitanism assumes education and travel, the wherewithal of the breaking of traditions, things noncosmopolitan have often been assumed to characterize the lower classes.[7] In his account of the lower-class music hall of Edwardian England, for example, Pearsall suggests that songs which reflected the experiences of the subaltern urban classes comprised the urban folk songs of the era:

> The songs lived on after their creators and exploiters were dead. The songs somehow embodied the sentiments and feelings of the submerged classes, and the idea that music hall song was the only true urban folk art gained credence throughout the Edwardian period. (Pearsall, 1975: 58)

Ephemeral songs have proved to be those tied to fads and contemporary events; those which express aspects of working-class life have lasted. Over a period of time, the words seem to be retained accurately — perhaps suggesting their importance — while the

melodies become subject to great variation, with the same infor-
mant often unable to sing a folk song twice the same way. Quite
distinct are the peasant folk songs, the bourgeois social songs, and
the industrial folk songs. The industrial folk song contains many
occupation-related references, often in a glossary not understood
outside the occupation; it served as a precursor to the industrial
protest song, often reflecting occupational hazards (Lloyd, 1967:
16, 316ff., 319–321, 323).

However, it is not necessarily the presence of a lower stratum
that serves as the social basis of folk music. It is the lettered who
most faithfully preserve folk songs, especially in peasant or rural
societies which have grass-roots traditions of learnedness. Throughout Europe peasants have had family song books which preserved
folk music in written form through generations. Peasants have also
used published collections of folk songs (Lloyd, 1967: 22, 25).
Thus, folk music may be seen to be as much the product of the
meeting between local, lower-class traditions and cosmopolitanism
as anything else. Just as no class exists in isolation but only through
a comparison with some other class, a stratum-based musical genre
such as folk music emerges when members of the lower class
reflect on their culture with some other class in mind.

III. NATIONALISM AND THE HISTORICAL BLOC

The phenomenon of people identifying with nation states is a
modern one. In its crudest form it impels populations into wars
against one another and leads them to accept the ethically indefen-
sible slogan, "My country right or wrong!" In less crude forms, it
calls upon individuals to transcend selfish and narrow interests for
the common good. In either instance a degree of personal worth
and selfhood has often been tied up with nationalism and national
feeling. The musical reflections of nationalism are frequently
obvious, particularly in martial music used by parade bands on
national holidays.

Paradoxically, the age of nationalism was and is also the age
of individualism. Beginning with the cult of reason and profit in
the Italian Renaissance, which was prefigured by Scholastic intel-
lectualism, the traditional and localistic bases of Western cultures
gave way to rationalism and cosmopolitanism. The admirable and
dependable person was no longer the one who preserved customs
but the one who acted on the grounds of objective, universally

recognizable reasoning. This historical tendency was most expressly evident in the French Revolution of 1789, in which localities and traditions within France were de-emphasized or suppressed in favor of reasoned substitutes. Departments replaced provinces, metric measures replaced customary ones, metric money replaced traditional monies. A large, universal administrative center was needed to serve as the guarantor of the new order, and with the failure of Napoleon's empire and later of Britain's and France's colonial empires, the nation state became the surrogate for tradition's eternal past.

The new national orders entailed the diminishing of clan, tribal, and regional influences. The freedom to act rationally on the part of the individual required a powerful national state which could overrule the extended family, the community, and the tribe. Placing too much power in the state, however, would again limit the freedom of the individual. Thus the nation state era marked an inherent social contradiction between the individual and the state. The strength of the state depends on individuals who are relatively free from rival sources of political power, but the freedom and individuality of those persons stand in contrast to the level of unfreedom upon which the state is founded.

The atomized, unattached individual was not merely a troublesome political necessity for the nation state. The new order was an economic one as well. The modern world is that of the industrial revolution as much as of the French Revolution. In the new economic order, large commercial enterprises create profits for the owners (state or private) out of the work of a force of laborers. Sufficient insight on the part of labor into the internal workings of this structure could bring such a system to an abrupt if contested halt. One way of hiding the situation from the laborer has been entirely economic — allowing profits to accrue from scarcity and inflation rather than from full production with profits resulting from low pay. In this strategem, labor's wage demands can be met, but production is kept down so that shortages create higher prices, which in turn create profits. The laborer comes up short as a consumer rather than as a wage earner.

The other way the workings of economic world is hidden from the laborer is to lead him or her to identify with the nation state. If the good of the state is equated with the good of the citizen, then the citizen can be convinced to think in terms of the nation rather than in terms of reasoned personal interest. Identifying with the state rather than, for instance, with an economic class, requires that there be some national culture in whose symbols the individual can feel at home. When this national culture is openly patriotic, its sociopolitical-economic consequences can be readily assessed. More subtle, however, is the national culture which is politically neutral, although it serves the purpose equally well. Following the terminology of the brilliant commentator upon Italian society of the early twentieth century, Antonio Gramsci, a culture which entices citizens away from their local concerns and thus makes local militancy for individual and class ends difficult thereby forms a "historical bloc" (see Portelli, 1972). What happens is that people of talent who emerge in the oppressed classes are recruited into a national culture rather than left in marginal areas to organize and articulate the viewpoint of the poor and exploited. In this respect music has at times been an important and unfortunate social influence.

Theodor Adorno has examined Wagner's *Die Meistersinger* as an allegory portraying the nationalism of nineteenth-century German businessmen (1976: ch. 10). In the opera a dreamy noble masters the cultural skills necessary for winning a singing contest sponsored by village businessmen. The cultural skill of singing thereby becomes the link between two social strata: noble and businessman. The plot has parallels with the German situation of the time, wherein the business class and the Prussian nobles, among others, were in the process of becoming unified in a new German polity. This cultural unity masked the fact that the businessmen had had no real efficacy in German politics since the failure of their revolution in 1848. Adorno notes that Wagner himself was a frustrated former revolutionary. He observes that not only the stories of Wagner's operas but the musical form that he used aspired to a sense of an all-encompassing totality which would render lesser peculiarities insignificant (1976: 118).

Many nineteenth-century composers consciously expressed national feeling in their music. It is also true, however, that music composed with no nationalistic feeling in mind could be put to use as a way of clouding class realities. John H. Mueller (1951: 200–210) credits the Bach revival of the nineteenth century not only to Felix Mendelssohn and Eduard Devrient's performance of the *St. Matthew's Passion* in Berlin in 1829 but also to a then incipient German nationalism. Bach had long been the musicians' composer, as opposed to an audience pleaser, and, according to Mueller, public appeal began to grow out of the Germans' interest in their own cultural history. J. S. Bach was, after all, a historical figure of whom the Germans could be proud.

When music or any other cultural form becomes a point of collective identity, an inherent conservatism is introduced into it. The composer is no longer free to use the total universe of sound combinations or to avoid clichés. Thus the traditionalism of patriotic music and the innovativeness of art music may be seen as dialectically related aspects of the same process occurring in cultural history (see the section "Schoenberg and Progress" in Adorno, 1973).

A contemporary variety of the historical bloc is the formation of a collective identity with popular music. In the previous section it was shown that mass culture may not provide the unity that some supposed; for instance, different kinds of popular music reinforced class divisions among English adolescents. Nevertheless, popular music has certainly blurred class lines in many instances, enabling far different people to express a false unity in their identifying with the same cultural form. Adorno's description of American popular music (1976: 25-26) suggests that a certain authoritarianism is implicit in this cultural unity. The music never changes, despite superficial variations. Each generation, even when cultivating a peculiar style or variety of pop music, identifies with a rigid formula of thirty-two bars with a "bridge" (a part initiating the repetition) in the middle. The listeners bow to the eternal formula while individualizing their preferences for certain precalculated effects that are thrown in to add spice to the sameness.

In order to have an adequate grasp of the "historical bloc," as exemplified in the dynamics of popular music, it is necessary to contrast it to the "mass culture" concept. The mass culture theory held that the old patterns of cultural diversity would disappear, that differences along ethnic, regional, and class lines would diminish. The old differentiated collection of musical cultures would give way to a cultural uniformity. In the historical bloc approach, the sociologist sees the potential leaders of the underclasses coopted out of the ranks of those who need them and into the ranks of a cultural elite. The cultural elite need not, however, be connoisseurs of serious music; in fact, serious music may require more childhood opportunity than a potential leader of the disadvantaged is likely to have had. Thus for the formation of a historical bloc there would need to be another elite culture running parallel to that of serious music and crossing various class lines though leaving some behind.[8]

Elite cultural expressions sometimes engender their opposite: non-elite cultural expressions. For instance, intellectualized official religions sometimes engender popular or folk religious forms. Similarly, serious elite music may be doubled by an unserious, designedly unelite music. In the United States, "country music" seems to be a double of that kind. First identified with lower-class rural-to-urban migrants from inner America, especially from the South, it has spread to non-country people who are white and between twenty-five and forty-nine, who have little education, and who hold working-class occupations (Peterson and di Maggio, 1975). That is to say, it has crossed some old regional and ethnic divides thus attaining a deliberately non-elite status. Historically, however, it has not attained the full potential of a class expression because it has not crossed racial lines and has not accorded itself the dignity of seriousness. In addition, it does not hide relevant class divides; and therefore has not provided a historical bloc. Country music, perhaps, is a case of an incomplete populism, neither bridging nor forging class expressions.

IV. RATIONALIZATION AND MUSIC

Antonio Gramsci (1975: 58ff.), writing from one of Mussolini's prisons in the 1920s and 1930s observed that everyone is a philosopher. It is not only the academic specialist in philosophy who has a world view but each person forms an intellectual world. The difference between the majority of people and academic philosophers is that most people's views lack the coherence and system which formal philosophies have. Most people's general views are influenced by such diverse factors as language, what is accepted in their locality as common sense, popular religion, and folklore. The language may be expressive, full of exclamations, or it may be replete with clichés and ambiguities. One need only interview a group of average people in public polling or survey work to see how much trouble they have following formal language. It is not a matter of their not understanding some of the words, though that could happen too, but of their not understanding the way concepts are linked together in long sentences and paragraphs. Or "common sense" to them may be a mere matter of habit and local custom, and may include prejudices. Popular religion and folklore may seem superstitious at times and sophisticated at other times. As a result the average person's philosophy may be self-contradictory, not systematized, not organized by reason. Gramsci wanted to bring the skills and habits of reason and critical analysis to the common people. Sociologists refer to the process of spreading these skills and habits to new aspects of the cultural world as *rationalization.*

The "modern world," which is a smaller entity than the universe of everything recent, is characterized by rationality. To be modern is to severely limit the arational, perhaps even driving it out of one's leisure time. Planning and organization overrule spontaneity and tradition. Some commentators may use the term *rational* differently, holding that mental forms which are inadequate for encompassing the spontaneous and traditional aspects of reality are not in fact rational, but the more limited meaning is intended in the present discussion.[9] In music it involves specialization and reasoning. Specialization entails a division of labor wherein musicians and composers can devote all of their working hours to music so that they can develop the necessary specialized skills and knowledge. Reasoning entails an ordering of the music by stylistic rules and principles (e.g., the classical rules of harmony and the contemporary methods of purposely deviating from them).

An unintended consequence of the rationalization of music is the reinforcement or encouragement it gives to the rationalization process in general. If an off-hours, nonbusiness pursuit such as listening to music reveals plan and order to the listener, plan and order per se may seem to be more natural than they actually are. Thus, the planned and ordered industrial world seems to be natural and, hence, acceptable. Our customary polyphonic form of music has even been seen as a legitimating reflection of the general division of labor in society (Adorno, 1973: 18).

Whatever the connection may be between rationalization of the social world on the one hand, including such important aspects of it as economic organization, and the rationalization of music on the other, there are always arational influences as well. The religious mentality, set apart from the mental containers and chains of discursive reasoning, has engendered much musical composition and performance. The music market, so important in the romantic movement, in opera, and in popular music, is certainly a factor which stands outside of musical rationality, though it involves business rationality. Thus, the rationalization of music, wherein principles are formulated and used to give system to the music, has occurred in private spheres, protected from nonmusical influences. The developmental logic of music, taking it along a path of increasing intellectualization, has been worked out above all in chamber music (Adorno, 1976: 92).

It is not a matter of chamber music having no social aspect. As a form of interaction it can be understood as a retreat from the competitive world. Unlike market music and audience-oriented music, it thrives in a private sphere. In contrast to the star system, the individuals step back to allow a whole to emerge. It might even be seen as a critique of the world-as-contest (Adorno, 1976: 86–92). The point is that in this relatively private sphere, where musical form is the only consideration, the rationalization of music has proceeded at the fastest pace.

In his study of musical rationality, Max Weber found rationality existing in a dialectical relationship with irrationality.

> Chordal rationalization lives only in continuous tension with melodism, which it can never completely devour. Chordal rationalization also conceals in itself an irrationality due to the unsymmetrical position of the seventh, unsymmetrical in terms of distance. (Weber, 1958: 10)

Perhaps compositional developments since Weber's time may be seen as attempts to eliminate the dialectic (see Malhotra, 1979). In any case the rationalization process seemed to Weber to be a concomitant of music evolving into a profession. The rationalization of harmony in particular has structured Western hearing. Even atonal music depends for its effect upon its contrast to the tonal principles (Weber, 1958: 41, 102).

If one approaches rationality from a relativist position, the appearance of coherence and logic may be questioned. One person's reason may be another's chaos. Since each person's reason is something close to the very self, it is inevitably entangled in the matter of identity. That is, each person identifies with a rationality. As identities differ, so do rationalities. Thus, the matter of rationality is related to that of nationality and of the historical bloc. Indeed, in the previous section it was shown that in the phenomenon of the "historical bloc" it was the systemic and reasoned (i.e., rationalized) cultural forms which recruit potential underclass leaders into a transethnic, supra-class elite. Rationalization may thus be seen as an aspect of the structure of society, a mark of the formation of a cultural elite co-opted out of revolution and other forms of class-relevant, practical conduct. However private the sphere of musical rationalization, it is not without its public implications.

V. MUSIC, MOVEMENTS, AND THE UNDERDOG

Social movements occur when a large number of ordinary people become convinced that something must be changed in their world and proceed to act on their conviction. Sometimes they create formal organizations to further their objectives, but such organizations themselves are only viable when they are supported by an active sector of society. Furthermore, social movements occur when there is opposition to the change which the movement seeks to effect. There would be no need for a movement if there were no opposition; it would be a matter of legislating an uncontroversial law or disseminating some uncontested information. A social movement thus involves a change of consciousness, where a social sector becomes aware of a large-scale wrong and seeks to convert other sectors of society to its awareness and assessment of the situation. This is often as much a matter of a change of values and interpretations as it is of the spread of information. Because social elites tend to dominate the values and interpretations characteristic of official cultures, social movements more often than not represent the views and desires of ethnic minorities, the disadvantaged, the disenchanted, and the "off beat," because the movements generally array against the dominant viewpoints.

These attributes of social movements are not arbitrary traits selected in advance to define social movements. They are the outcome of a social situation of which a social movement is a part. A movement does not emerge from a "bright idea" or even from a "charismatic leader," but rather is one side of a social complex; an idea "rings true" and a leader elicits a response when the larger social complex is made visible. The larger complex is the dynamic of social inequality. Classes of people are not born unequal; they must be made unequal for a system of inequality to persist. When an underdog class experiences the process of being made underdogs, they have the biographical potential of taking actions which would not only defend the victims of the inequality but also in the process offend the beneficiaries of inequality. Thus the opposition to a social movement is an essential aspect of the social movement situation. A complete account would note not only consciousness, goals, social movements and value changes, but also the reverse of these: anticonsciousness, antigoals, countermovements, and countervalues. These are all aspects of a situation in which what is good for one sector of society is bad for another.

Some of the best known social movements in modern history are the antislavery or abolitionist movement of the nineteenth century, the labor movement of the nineteenth and twentieth centuries, the civil rights movement of the twentieth century, and the antiwar movement of the twentieth century. Various revolutions, such as the American Revolution (1776–1781), the French Revolution (1789), and the European revolutions of 1848, might be seen as social movements which toppled governments or tried to topple governments in the process of attempting to achieve their social and economic objectives. Indeed, revolutions may be distinguished from coups by the fact that they emanate from social movements.

Music, much as every other cultural expression, becomes taken up in social movement situations. Sometimes it merely expresses underdog status, thereby serving to lead people to see themselves as underdogs — a necessary cognitive development which must precede movement consciousness. Sometimes music styles exemplify some values — ranging from informality where formality may be expected (or vice-versa) to equality in highly stratified societies — which accord with one or more social movements. In still other instances a musical form expresses the solidarity of a social sector which stands to benefit from a social movement. The more susceptible music is to being rationalized, the more the purely musical interests of a movement-related musical form will be at odds with all these extramusical concerns. Conflict and tension sometimes result from this. Finally, music may be used expressly to convey a partisan movement viewpoint; this is particularly the case with "songs of persuasion."

An example of music expressing an underdog status is found in the lyrics of the tangos of Carlos Gardel. From the turn of the century until World War I the tango was a form of dance music common only in such South American cities as Buenos Aires and Montevideo; it had no lyrics, or at most only short, risque ones. During World War I, however, the tango moved upward in social status and outward, from the underclass and brothel societies of the cities of South America to international popularity. From 1918 to his death in 1939, Gardel was its most popular interpreter, and his versions included lyrics, usually depicting a man talking to himself, more often than not about a lost love. A number of sad biographical details were related; the narrator in the songs fatalistically endures these defeats, having no control over conditions. Economic defeat was often seen as preventing amorous success (Canton, 1968). North American blues might also be considered "underdog music." The consciousness stemming from such music might be seen as preliminary to social movements.

It was noted above that music might also exemplify values which accord with one or more social movements, or which pose an alternative to the dominant value systems. David Riesman once observed the presence of a "minority position"[10] in popular music listening among American youth. The "majority attitude" accepted the adult stereotype of youth and with it the commercial music which adults produced for youth. Conformity to this majority attitude entailed a state of mind in which experiences appear fleetingly, disconnected from one another. Accordingly, the popular music product "is presented disconnectedly, especially over the radio — where it is framed by verbal ballyhoo and atomized into individual 'hits.'" This music and the mentality deemed appropriate for youth were doubled by a minority attitude, which used non-star, non-brand name, "off beat" music to establish a distance from the majority culture. Significantly, this minority tended to favor underdogs in general and to take the progressive side of certain class and racial issues (Riesman, 1957). More recently, the rock concert setting of the 1960s exemplified alternative values; it was not a matter of rebellion but of adopting some attitudes deemed somewhat deviant and ignoring for a while generally approved attitudes (Dees, 1972: 219).

"Soul music" more openly expresses the solidarity of a social sector which stands to benefit from a social movement, specifically the black citizenry of the United States. The black musician has long served as a reminder of the fact that blacks can succeed where opportunity is to be found; thus, the black musician has held a political and social significance (see Kaplan, 1951: 196). With soul music, that potential has been made explicit. Although jazz in general developed as an accommodation of black and white musical traditions, soul music developed within the jazz world as a reassertion of black identity.[11] It represents a reaction within the musical world as well as within the wider social world, for despite the interracial appeal of soul, the bands which have played it have been largely segregated institutions. Soul music has served black musicians as a strategem for reserving a part of the employment market for themselves. In terms of a wider cultural significance, the soul music movement has capitalized on the stereotype of the black as having a "natural" talent for music (Szwed, 1966). Radio audience surveys showed that soul music has appealed to a younger generation of black listeners, who reject blues as expressing too much old-fashioned sadness and hopelessness (Haralambos, 1970).

As music takes on political or social significance, a conflict may develop between musical imperatives and nonmusical ones. Such a conflict was evidenced in the conducting career of Arturo Toscanini when he insisted on playing "German" music (Mozart, Wagner, etc.) in Italy during World War I, amidst much opposition, and when he refused to play the Fascist anthem at the beginning of concerts during the Mussolini era (see Taubman, 1951). With the specialization and rationalization of music, a desire to bring a musical genre to its fulfillment and to focus on it alone provides momentum to a process of depoliticization (see Bensman and Gerver, 1958). In the case of "German" music and resisting the Fascist idea of repertory, it was a matter of keeping nationalism and politics out of music. Particularly in the Fascist incident, it was a matter of keeping an overbearing state out of artistic decision-making. But the reverse has also been known to happen – political music, songs of persuasion, have been taken out of politics by people who found them musically interesting. In the early 1950s in San Francisco, a leftist political group which made great use of folk music experienced a split over the matter, a split into a political group and a folk music group (Arlene Kaplan, 1955).

The most direct use of music in social movements occurs when movement participants use songs of persuasion to sway public opinion, express a public stand, or reinforce their own solidarity with the movement in question. The original composer or songwriter may not have had such use in mind, or it may indeed have been the original intent. In either case the critical factor which makes a work a song of persuasion is the use to which it is put. Songs of persuasion may refer to a problem around which a movement has organized, or the songs may call for support for the movement itself. Sometimes they may ridicule the movement's opponents. In any case such songs are clearly message music (Denisoff, 1966).

In the United States songs of persuasion as a social form had their origins in religious revivals. In the eighteenth and early nineteenth centuries the music of revivalists' camp meetings was imitated by abolitionists, unionists, populists, socialists, and others. Later in the urban areas, the Salvation Army and the Wobblies used brass bands against one another, with the Wobblies making satirical parodies of religious music (Denisoff, 1970). The twentieth-century American left evinced diverse kinds of songs of persuasion. While the Granters and Populists used the style and fervor of fundamentalist religious hymns, the socialists added lyrics to more widely known religious melodies. The Workers party, the Independent Socialist League, and the Socialist Workers party — three Trotskyite groups — differed markedly from others in seeming to be amusical, while the Communists took to folk music (Denisoff, 1971: 5-9).

The Communists' effort to use folk music was an unusual phenomenon. The northern working class which the Communists were trying to reach in America in the 1930s were immigrants and descendants of immigrants from Europe. Most of the twenty thousand party members did not speak English easily or at all. Moscow ordered them to take up genuinely American art forms as a way of breaking out of their ethnic ghettos, but why folk music, which sounded exotic to the northern workers, was selected is hard to understand. Perhaps it was a matter of simple extension of the Russian experience, wherein the revolutionists addressed an illiterate and multiethnic populace through folk arts, and perhaps it reflected Stalin's partiality for folk music. Needless to say, it did not succeed in urban America in the thirties (Denisoff, 1971: 6-15).

The folk music of the American Southeast did address social problems, but with a conservative and escapist mentality. The Communists' first contact with it was during the Gastonia, North Carolina mill strike of 1929. The strikers' singer, Ella May Wiggins, became a martyr after vigilantes assassinated her, and people throughout the nation who identified with the union cause took to her music. A similar spread of strike ballads in the folk style was occasioned by the coal strikes in Harlan and Bell Counties, Kentucky, in the early 1930s. Communists were involved because traditional unions had failed, and the Communists' folk music policy brought the music northward. Meanwhile, folk music of persuasion was developing in labor colleges of the South which were attempting to raise the consciousness of southern workers and to train leaders. A black preacher who improvised on spirituals at Commonwealth Labor College in Mena, Arkansas, influenced two leftist songwriters, Lee Hays and John Handcox. The Brookwood Labor College at Katonah, New York, which the Communists did not approve of, engaged in considerable organizing activity in the South. Tom Tippett, who had a United Mine Workers background, provided Brookwood people with musical guidelines for use in the South. The Highlander Folk School in Monteagle, Tennessee was founded with the intention of using folk culture for social and economic purposes; its music, collected or composed by Mrs. Zilphia Horton, comprised some eleven songbooks. "We Shall Overcome" was disseminated through Highlander; and "We Shall Not Be Moved" was a negro spiritual adapted by the Southern Tenant Farmers Union, founded by Norman Thomas Socialists in 1934; it too was disseminated through Highlander. Although the Communists did establish a folk music organization in the 1930s, the better-known efforts of the Almanac Singers and of Woody Guthrie benefited the CIO rather than the Communist party, if increased membership is taken as any measure. While the Almanac Singers, with Guthrie, Pete Seeger, Lee Hays, and Millard Lampell at the core of the group, continued to promote Stalinist ideology through the 1940s, other folk singers, such as Burl Ives and Leadbelly, proved to be more interested in commercial success, which did not really come for some time (Denisoff, 1971: 18–36, 63–64, 71–88). Alan Lomax collected the material that generally set the folk repertory through the forties, and Paul Robeson perhaps reached the widest audience with it in his radio broadcasts.

The folk music revival of the 1960s was as much a reaction against commercial rock as a protest phenomenon (Lund and Denisoff, 1971). Nevertheless, it certainly turned toward persuasion briefly as an expression of the civil rights movment and the antiwar movement. The connection between the folk music and protest was probably accidental, since folk music first enjoyed commercial success with the Kingston Trio and later turned to persuasion. Presumably, if some other form of music had been popular, it too would have been used in the same way. Thus there was as much discontinuity as continuity between the work of people such as the Almanac Singers and the protest music of thirty years later.

4
Illustrative Studies

I. COSTUMING PERFORMERS

While music itself exists only as an interaction, a process in which one actor influences others and is influenced by them, it also exists amid other interactions. Sometimes it occurs within the setting of those exchanges which comprise a friendship group or a party, and music as a social phenomenon must be understood in that context. Sometimes it is within the formal ceremony of a political, religious, military, or commemorative occasion. Sometimes it is in the half-commercial, half-ritual ambient of the art music concert hall. In all of these interaction settings, the costumes of the participants serve as signs which help establish the relevant social framework.

The clothing of the participants helps establish a continuity with other occasions which the one in progress is supposed to resemble (Stone, 1965: 220). When the instrumentalists wear black tuxedos and long black dresses, an implicit social analogy is made with many other concert occasions. When the instrumentalists march by in brightly colored, quasi-military uniforms, continuity is established with football games and holiday parades. When the instrumentalists appear in a uniform patterned after a flashy and costly dress style much in vogue among youth, continuity is established with classy dance scenes. Costuming helps establish the occasional context for the music by implicitly introducing a body of cultural, historical, and social connotations and preventing what some would take to be incongruities (Goffman, 1961: 24).

The clothing and other props also help establish the identities of participants. Art music female soloists, for example, stand out from the non-soloists when they do not wear black. Pop vocalists similarly may dress differently from their accompanying musicians, and they may hold microphones. Musical groups will try to establish visual trademarks which have the effect of announcing their general musical genre as well as their identity. The individuals and small groups try to "look the part."

106

In addition to establishing continuity with known types of occasions and establishing participant identities, costuming also establishes the intended relationship between performer and audience (Stone, 1965: 222). In art music concerts, the audience is more or less well-dressed; hence, the performers, on whom attention is to be focused, are not only well-dressed but formally dressed. It is not so much a matter of being superior as establishing a ritual distance from the audience — somewhat in the manner of judicial, academic, and religious ceremonials. In contrast, commercial youth music minimizes the social distance between performer and audience. The performers must be young, use the language in vogue among the young, conduct themselves as if they do not quite know how to behave in public, and dress like the audience. The commercial success of the endeavor depends in part on giving the audience an anonymous power by conforming to it.

Bluegrass Costuming

The garb of twentieth-century bluegrass musicians in the United States provides an interesting illustration of some of the dynamics involved in musicians' clothing. The early twentieth-century rural music of the Southeast string band tradition had two distinct varieties, one representing something of a sacred tradition and one representing a profane one (see Malone, 1968). On the sacred side, there were groups, often composed of family members, who based their singing style on that found in rural fundamentalist churches. Often using two-, three-, or four-part harmony, they sang songs of God, home, faith, virtue, and tragedy. Their performances were serious and their clothing reflected this mood, often what can be described as "Sunday-go-to-meeting-clothes" — suits and ties for the men and modest dresses for the women. On the profane side, the music was based directly on the square dance tradition of the southern mountains, with the fiddle (the "instrument of the devil") playing hot tunes which, with seeming magic, would set people to dancing. This music was anything but serious and was often punctuated with the whoops and shouts of the performers and audience. It was from this side particularly that the term *hillbilly* became synonymous with early country music. Coveralls, red bandanas, bare feet, straw hats, and self-deprecating humor (much of which can be traced to the medicine show performers) were common.

A third variety had extraneous roots but was sometimes

present just the same in early country music; it was the "cowboy" or western type. Later in the century this type came to dominate the country music industry. Jimmy Rodgers, of course, was one of the first major stars of country music, and although he was born in Mississippi he appealed to the West by wearing a cowboy hat and boots. While these three are the ideal or pure types, most country music performers represent intermediary varieties.

Through the 1930s all three trends, in both pure and mixed form, could be found in country music imagery, with the western emphasis increasing as time went by. By the early 1940s, a number of individual performers were singing and playing music with western themes and dressing in western clothes. Although there had been a few cowboy singers and western bands in the 1920s, Jimmy Rodgers and then Gene Autry provided significant models for the western singer. Frequently from Texas, Oklahoma, and other southwestern states, the western musical groups gained popularity among the general country music audience and contributed to a change in country music. With the emergence of "honky-tonk music" instrumentation changed, the electric guitar, drums, and bass fiddle being added. The style of performance became harder; it was louder and marked by a more accentuated beat. The content of the lyrics became more realistic and less concerned with a bucolic rural past. While the string band tradition continued, the 1940s saw the clear rise of country-and-western music and a change in audience. As the music industry in Nashville sought to widen its market, the harsh, nasal singing style so common to the string band was replaced by a smoother, mellower singing style, such as that of Eddy Arnold, which was more acceptable to the "pop" music audience. In addition, the rural, illiterate country bumpkin suggested by the term *hillbilly* and by the farm-style clothes was also seen as a hindrance to the acquisition of a broader, more urban audience. Although the term *hillbilly* would not die out immediately, efforts began in the late 1940s to replace it with "country" or "country and western" (Malone, 1968: 210).

The development of bluegrass music can be located in the band organized by Bill Monroe during the last half of the 1940s. The costumes worn by Monroe and his band had been distinctive since he joined the Grand Ole Opry in 1939. While he and his brothers wore suits and ties, costumes on the Opry were generally more informal and country-flavored. Reportedly, Monroe's group was the first to perform wearing white shirts and ties (Rooney, 1971). In addition, the band regularly wore jodhpurs and riding boots and narrow-brimmed Stetson hats, suggestive of country gentlemen rather than hicks and yokels. Although one member of the band would often assume the role of a comic, the appearance and manner of the Blue Grass Boys indicated that the music was to be taken seriously.

By the end of the 1940s, Earl Scruggs and Lester Flatt, the first a banjoist and the second a vocalist and guitarist, had left Monroe's group to form their own highly successful band. Ralph and Carter Stanley, from Virginia, also began to record songs in a manner very similar to that of Monroe's group. With these three groups and numerous others which followed Monroe, his type of musical group and performance pattern was becoming a distinctive style. The Stanley Brothers, Flatt and Scruggs, and many other bluegrass groups adopted clothing which was quite different from the obviously western style of most 1950s country music performers. Dressed in contemporary, unadorned suits, their concession to the western influence was in the regular use of string ties and western hats. With the exception of the comedian of such groups, there was little suggestive of the hillbilly in their appearance, and their manner was generally folksy but serious. It should be mentioned that Monroe dropped the riding breeches and boots by 1952, while retaining to the present white dress shirts and ties. In addition, Monroe's band began to wear wider-brimmed, western hats.

The brother-based bluegrass bands, the Osborne Brothers and Jim and Jessie (McReynolds), had groups with the traditional non-amplified instrumentation of the bluegrass band. In an appeal to a wider audience, both groups introduced the use of steel guitars and drums in their recordings and appearances, as well as electrified mandolins and occasionally electric guitars. With these musical changes, there were also changes in clothing. Jim and Jessie adopted obviously western-style clothes and the Osborne Brothers went so far as to order glittery suits, typical of many country-and-western performers. In an interview with one of the authors (Dees, May 1979) Sonny Osborne stated that they were trying to appeal to the broader country-and-western audience and that they felt the clothes would help symbolize this intention. These and other performers with a bluegrass background (such as Jimmy Martin) did in fact obtain some level of commercial success with this transition, but most have dropped the new instrumentation and changed their clothing style since the popularity of bluegrass began to increase dramatically.

In the late 1960s bluegrass music began enjoying a larger commercial success; bluegrass festivals were held throughout the country. In addition, an increasingly large number of young urban musicians from various parts of the country began to play the music and to experiment with modifications of it. Influenced by contemporary rock as well as by other popular music forms, many of these so-called "newgrass" performers have pushed the limits of the style established by Monroe. They use more complex progressions, electrical amplification, and less traditional material. The more extreme newgrass groups have, in fact, alienated many hardcore bluegrass devotees while simultaneously attracting the interest of listeners who previously had little interest in bluegrass. It should be emphasized that there are a number of other groups which, although experimental in comparison to Monroe, remained closer to the traditional style. Many of these groups no longer have a common costume for the group. They appear in everyday street clothes rather than a coordinated group uniform.

Costumes and Music: A Consideration of Function

For musicians who find themselves playing in settings over which they have little control, the means of establishing desired contexts is limited largely to appearance and manner. The use of various types of clothing by bluegrass musicians over three decades demonstrates that groups can borrow the costuming styles of other kinds of groups for such purposes as attracting wider audiences and harkening to real or mythical traditions.

In the case of the first musical group organized by Bill Monroe, the use of riding breeches and boots, along with white shirts and ties, conveyed a serious intention, and in this way countered the frivolous, illiterate, and lower-class image often associated with the fiddle and dance music of the string band tradition. Many of the desired connotations, of course, were drawn from the serious, "sacred" string band groups. The riding breeches and boots had apparently not been used previously in musical groups, but they were symbolic of the refinement of the Kentucky horseman.

The adoption of the western hat and tie by such groups as Flatt and Scruggs, the Stanley Brothers, and to some extent even by Monroe in the fifties, may be seen as an effort to represent an affiliation with country-and-western music, while simultaneously maintaining an independence through the use of nonwestern-style suits.

In the 1960s, the adoption of clearly western-style clothes, along with some instrumentation typical of the contemporary country-and-western band, represented an intentional effort to find acceptance in new settings and among country-and-western music's broader audience.

At present few groups, other than Monroe's band, perform in white shirts and ties, and there is in fact a generally casual kind of dress, which does little to distinguish the performer from the audience. The consequence of this, of course, is to suggest that the audience and performers are of equal status. Such an ideology is understandable in light of the very strong sentiment which holds that bluegrass music is an "authentic" folk idiom with little commercial contamination. Such a position, while quite appealing, is, of course, more myth than fact, since bluegrass has developed and flourished within a commercial context.

The symbolic value of clothing as complementary to an anticipated course of action suggests a typology of possible combinations of changes in musical performance and clothing. First, a double change — of clothing and of musical elements — represents an extreme innovation. Second, a modification of musical elements but a retention of an established clothing pattern symbolizes that the performers have not changed in their commitment to a previously established constituency. Third, a change of clothing without a change in music represents a change in the performer-audience relationship, perhaps the acquisition of a new audience.

II. SOCIAL FACTORS AND THE FIVE–STRING BANJO

In his analysis of the rationalization of music, the famous German sociologist Max Weber (1958) demonstrated that technical, social, and economic factors all contributed to the development of Western music as a rationalized system of activity in such areas as harmony, the twelve-tone scale, and instrumentation. This section is meant to illustrate the interaction of these various social factors in the development of playing styles for the five-string banjo. Banjo playing provides a convenient case in point because the development of its styles has taken place on the North American continent during the past two hundred years; its history is accessible.

The banjo originated as a crude folk instrument, related to a number of African, European, and Asian predecessors. The two hundred years in which it has developed have seen the rise of industrialism, invention of the mechanical reproduction of sound, and growth of the professional country musician as an occupational category. The banjo thus presents an unusually rich field for investigating how technical, social, and economic factors have bearing on the development of music.

An important part of Weber's analysis was his identification of the impact a developing stratum of professional musicians had on modern music history. The rise of such a stratum is described as furthering the sophistication of music by promoting a pattern of complementary actions leading to the rationalization of harmony and tone-interval rules (1958: 36-44). Weber noted that primitive music served either cultic or exorcistic purposes and thus was subject to traditional and evaluative actions which sought to preserve and use music's supposed magical powers. This conservative tendency paradoxically promoted progressive change by standardizing musical formulae. Experts in such fixed formulae were needed; hence, such conservativism indirectly gave rise to a body of professional musicians who were more interested in the music and its potential than in any extrageneric uses — magical or otherwise. An interest in the music itself in turn gave rise to experimentation and the shattering of the musical formulae. Thus, Weber identified two sets of actions — standardization and specialization — each associated with different purposes, which nevertheless jointly contributed to the rationalization of music.

Weber's analysis of musical development also considers the significance of musical instruments and their relationship with rationalization. Considering such instruments as the piano, organ, and violin, he identified the impact of improved methods of construction, the social groups and organizations which supported the use of particular instruments, the consequence of factory production and large-scale distribution of instruments, and the role of such instruments in music production. Weber noted that while some modifications of musical instruments were consequences of rationalizing activities in other areas of social life, many changes were first introduced in music itself for aesthetic purposes and rationalizing efforts followed later (1958:109-110).

We will examine the origin and evolution of the material construction of the five-string banjo in this light, and then examine the emergence of major styles of banjo playing within identifiable social contexts.[1] The main concern of the discussion will be the identification of rationalizing processes and the changing function of the banjo as a musical instrument.

History of the Banjo

The banjo is a type of long lute within the family of chordo-phones, instruments which produce sound by the vibration of strings which are under tension. Comprised principally of a neck and a resonant body, the banjo shares basic similarities with such instruments as the violin and sitar, and is even more similar to other lutes which are plucked with the fingers and which can be found in Africa, Asia, and the ancient Mediterranean (Reck, 1977: 123-131). The immediate ancestors of the banjo in North America were either brought over or procured by African slaves in the colonial period.[2] One of the earliest recorded observations of these instruments was made by Thomas Jefferson, who noted that a favorite instument of the slaves was the "banjar" (Jefferson, 1955). Other sources suggest that the instrument at this time was a crude affair, made from a gourd with strings of organic material.[3] This construction, easily adaptable to available resources, made the instrument accessible to slaves and allowed for the continuation of African musical traditions. The percussive sounds of these early banjos were used in the production of complex polyrhythms typ-ical of much African music as well as of the musical conventions which the slaves adopted from the music of the colonists. An example of this adaptation was the use of the instrument for the jig music of the British Isles.[4] In turn, the instrument was intro-duced to white members of American society, who found it com-patible with their own musical interests (see Bluestein, 1954; Epstein, 1975; Heaton, 1970).

As it gained popularity among white audiences and performers through its use in minstrel shows prior to the Civil War, the banjo was transformed into an instrument with standardized features. Just as the violin had undergone several material changes when a new social stratum began to use it (Weber, 1958: 106-107), the banjo was also subject to modification as a result of the technical traditions of the white population. The neck of the instrument began to resemble that of the guitar and lute, drum-type bodies were constructed, resonators were developed to reflect the sound toward the audience, and the number of strings was standardized at five. This last modification, popularly attributed to a well-known pre-Civil War minstrel performer,[5] would be a significant influence in the development of later playing styles. The fifth string, unlike the others, did not extend the entire length of the neck but terminated about two-thirds of the distance from the body; and although it was tuned to the highest pitch of all the strings, the fifth string was juxtaposed to the string tuned to the lowest pitch. In the last half of the nineteenth century, other changes were introduced, such as the use of frets, and the quality of construction improved as the instrument became widely popular and available to the general public through factory production and mail-order catalog distribution.[6] The rationalizing consequences of standardization in this context appeared in the development of popularly preferred ways of tuning and playing the instrument.

Banjo Playing Styles

The physical construction of any instrument imposes limits on the kinds of techniques which musicians may use. While minor modifications have been introduced to improve sound quality, the banjos of the latter part of the nineteenth century possessed the same basic potential for playing techniques as those produced today. That particular playing styles developed when and where they did is the major concern of the following discussion. A style is a predictable combination of features distinguishable from other styles (Rosenblum, 1978: 424). Each style can be located and made sense of within a specific social context and historical period; a style is not presumed to develop and spread by accident or fate.

Frailing Style

The frailing style is generally considered to be the oldest surviving technique of playing the banjo and to have developed from the playing of slaves. It relies on a downward movement of the back of the right hand across the strings. Although there are a number of variations of and other terms for this manner of playing, the basic frailing style was widely used in the latter part of the nineteenth century.[7] The distinctive sound of the frailing style is derived from fundamental movements of the right hand and the use of the fifth string for a droning sound.[8] In frailing, the right hand makes three basic movements. The back or nail side of the middle finger strikes downward on one of the higher strings; second, the middle finger and possibly others strike downward again, but hit several strings; finally, the thumb plucks the fifth string with a movement toward the inside of the palm. The standardization of this technique produces a distinctive rhythmic effect in which the first note is equal in time to the values of the next two combined, resulting in the production of a "galloping" or "boom-diddy" effect — an eighth note followed by two sixteenth notes. The melody of a song is played primarily by the first movement, while the remaining movements contribute a rhythmic and harmonic background. The use of the thumb in plucking the fifth string is particularly important in this context, in that while the four longer strings may be fretted or noted for particular tones, the fifth string is unchanged, acting as a drone. While the use of drone strings is not uncommon in stringed instruments around the world, the fifth string of the banjo is thought to have provided a substitute for the drone of the bagpipe found in European music. Frailing was particularly well suited for jig music, which frequently inserted a rest in the first half of a measure to "weaken" it (Nathan, 1962: 205).

The fingers of the left hand were used to stop the strings at those positions which would allow the production of desired melody notes and tones to form chords. However, because many nineteenth-century banjos did not have frets, precise noting was difficult and seldom occurred beyond the location of the fifth string on the neck. In order to accommodate the modal tunes of British traditional music, modal tunings developed for the banjo which would allow the performer to follow more closely the melody line. Over one hundred such tunings have been identified, and some of these seem to have been used for just one or two particular songs.[9]

Although the banjo was quite popular in the United States and England during the last half of the nineteenth century, and the subject of numerous attempts to standardize playing techniques and tunings, it was most securely established in the mountainous regions of the rural South.[10] The percussive, bounding sounds of the banjo complemented the fiddle, and these two instruments became identified with dance music; they were often viewed by members of the puritanical "respectable society" as "instruments of the devil." Frailing remained the dominant style for southeastern musicians well into the twentieth century and may still be found in the rural Southeast today. The popularity of the frailing style may be understood by examining the social context within which it was used. Although dancing was condemned by the more fundamentalist religious groups of the South, the highly expressive dancing of the British jig tradition survived in the more isolated mountains. Both those who played this music and those who banned it recognized the apparent magical power it had to move people to dance. The association of this power with the devil is evident in such traditional tunes as "Devil's Dream" and "Up Jumped the Devil." This antagonism of religious and aesthetic experience has been described by Weber as producing for the religious individual a sign of the "diabolical nature of art" (Weber, 1946: 342). Evidence of the aversion of the "respectable" segments of southern society to the music of the fiddle and banjo may still be found today in the ordinances of many southern towns which prohibit "common fiddlers" and other common musicians from remaining in the city limits after nightfall. The use of these instruments was never banned completely, however, and they were frequently used by performers with traveling medicine shows and even among the "play parties" of the more conservative religious groups in the community.[11]

Other reasons for the popularity of the frailing style and of the banjo in general may be found in the characteristics of the style and of the construction of the banjo itself. Frailing depends on a few basic movements, which, once mastered, can be used for accompaniment of other voices and for a limited statement of the melody line. Because of its simplicity, the style does not require extensive training; hence it was adaptable for rural musicians who might spend the better part of their days in hand, manual labor. This basic codified form represents a level of simple rationalization which could be easily transmitted from one individual to another, and which was disseminated by traveling musicians. In addition, the instrument is far more durable than the guitar and the violin, thereby rendering it less susceptible to damage in a rough environment, in contrast to an indoor instrument such as the piano (see Weber, 1958: 122).

The promotion of the banjo and of frailing by professional musicians in the South was limited to those performers to be found in the traveling medicine shows and in some larger communities. In fact, commercial music through the first two decades of the twentieth century was primarily urban-oriented (Malone, 1968: 33) because of the low financial gain which performers and promoters expected from rural ventures. The technical development of radio broadcasting and the "discovery" of country music by the record industry in the 1920s changed this situation and promoted the emergence of the professional musician in the South. Malone (1968: 35-40) argues that these developments created new occupational possibilities for performers who could meet the new demand of a rural mass market. Once-isolated playing styles and songs were soon made available to people geographically dispersed, and country music was subjected to the rationalizing consequences of "refinement, modification, and eventual standardization." One performer who played the banjo in the frailing style at the critical transition time was David Harrison Macon. Professionally known as "Uncle Dave," Macon joined the Grand Ole Opry in 1926 (the program was one year old at the time) at the age of fifty-six. A singer and comedian, Macon was more of an entertainer than a virtuoso, setting a pattern for frailing banjoists which has continued to recent years in the careers of performers such as the late Dave "Stringbean" Akeman and Louis "Grandpa" Jones. Whether playing as a soloist or a member of a string band (usually fiddle, guitar, banjo, and mandolin), the banjoist would primarily act as a source of rhythmic and harmonic accompaniment for other instruments or voices and provide comic relief within a musical program. The regular association of the comic role and the frailing banjo style may be taken as an indication that the instrument was not seriously considered as a virtuoso instrument.

It should be mentioned briefly that there were attempts to develop a playing style in the northeastern United States which might establish the banjo as a "serious" instrument. In the latter part of the nineteenth and early part of the twentieth century, professional stage musicians attempted to make banjo adaptations of techniques used in classical guitar style. Classical banjo style, as it was called, was popular among stage performers and some of the public and relied on stiff, formalized movements of the fingers of the right hand to produce tremolos and cadenzas. Several professional banjoists composed songs for the instrument and wrote instruction books, but dissemination of the style was largely limited to the northeastern parts of the United States and to England.[12] Although the banjo was used in some ensembles as a chamber instrument, it eventually lost popularity as other, louder instruments assumed lead melodic roles and the four-string tenor banjo was developed to provide a louder, rhythmic accompaniment for music ensembles. Despite the decline of the classical style, it has survived in some areas of the U.S., but largely as a type of art form which is preserved for its "antique" quality. It should be noted, however, that as Weber found in the case of the evolution of string instruments (1958: 106-107), attempts to promote the classical style occurred as a result of efforts by professional musicians.[13]

Although the frailing style was most popular among banjoists of the South, other styles, both idiosyncratic and more broadly shared, were also present. Apparently existing primarily in North and South Carolina (Heaton, 1970), these styles used the thumb and first finger or first two fingers of the right hand to pluck the strings. Such techniques, probably influenced by classical guitar and banjo styles, produced a more distinctive sounding of each string than allowed in the frailing style. These personal styles, which allowed the banjoist to play part of the melody line, were occasionally used in the string band groups of the 1930s and 1940s, but insofar as they did not rest on the codified, standardized system of technical rules of performance, they promoted individual experimentation rather than a rationalization of technique.[14] In addition, these finger-picking styles were not based on the smooth flowing series of notes, and the rhythmically irregular sounds which they often produced were not always compatible with ensemble performance. It was out of these various efforts, however, that the next distinctive style emerged.

Scruggs Style

This widely popular style of banjo playing is named after Earl Scruggs, who is credited with its popularization. It uses the thumb and first two fingers of the right hand and is based on a series of patterned movements commonly called rolls. Within these rolls the thumb and fingers strike various strings as is appropriate for the melody. The notes picked are rapid, usually four to each beat of the music (typically sixteenth notes), and largely derived from chord positions formed by the left hand. Through a combination of various rolls, chord changes, and selective playing of the strings, a banjoist using the Scruggs style can achieve a series of rapidly flowing notes which follow the melody in a general fashion, and any superfluous notes (not present in the melody, but produced through the use of the rolls) would be harmoniously compatible. As was the case with frailing, the Scruggs style uses the fifth string as a drone, usually playing the tonic, through all chord changes. Consequently, the Scruggs style, with its performance of a melody line within a continuous series of notes with a steady syncopation, requires that the performer perfect the ability to make smooth, rapid, and accurate right-hand finger movements. The precision needed in the Scruggs style requires a greater delicacy of movement than that needed in the frailing style and generally requires more effort for mastery.

The popularity of the Scruggs style is historically linked with the development of bluegrass music in the years immediately following World War II, when Earl Scruggs joined the Blue Grass Boys headed by Kentuckian Bill Monroe. A mandolinist, Monroe had been a member of a string band with his brothers before organizing his own band in the late 1930s. String bands were vocal and instrumental groups which played the traditional music of the southern mountains, particularly in the adjoining areas of eastern Tennessee, Kentucky, southwestern Virginia, and western North Carolina. The vocal style of the singers in this area was a "treble, tight-throated rubato parlando, irregular and highly ornamented" (Rosenbaum, 1968: 24). The most common instruments in the string bands were the guitar and mandolin, with frequent additions of fiddle, banjo, and autoharp. In most string bands, instrumental virtuosity was not particularly stressed, and instrumental passages were typically performed in unison. Vocally, a close two-part harmony was very common in the string bands, although it was not unusual to find vocal performances in unison. With the sudden demand for country music produced by the appearance of radio stations in the South and the "discovery" of the market for country music by the phonograph industry, a great many string bands appeared, often composed of neighbors and family members.[15] Thus, the rising market for commercial music provided economic incentives for recording companies and radio stations to seek out country musicians. In turn, many rural and southern musicians found in music an opportunity for employment and possible upward mobility. Typical of many of the "brother" groups of the 1920s through the 1940s, Bill Monroe and his two brothers performed as an ensemble in various parts of the midwestern and southern United States. In addition to the influence of British music traditions, these brother groups also borrowed from Afro-American music, particularly the use of "blues notes" (flatted fifths and sevenths).[16] Finally, it should be recalled that the expansion of the radio and recording industry in the South also promoted the exposure of southern musicians to the commercial products which were made in other parts of the country and world.

In 1945, when Earl Scruggs joined Monroe's group, the country music industry had developed a mass audience and a variety of musical orientations. While mountain-style string bands were still to be found, there was also the western image popularized by Jimmy Rodgers and cowboy singers. In place of the many regionally based vocal styles, a new, smoother singing style had developed, which was attractive to urban audiences, and electric instruments were replacing the acoustic instruments of the early string bands.[17] Many of the older string bands had disappeared, and the term *western* was being used more frequently to describe the music, rather than the *hillbilly* label, which seemed to imply a backwoods, uneducated, and undesirable image. In the mid-forties, the honky-tonk songs dominated country music, and young bands which attempted to maintain the older, mountain styles found competition difficult. Bill Monroe's band was one of several which sought to compete with the new, "slick" image of Nashville.

Since forming his band in 1938, Monroe had attempted to incorporate a number of characteristics which would be commercially successful. In addition to the vocal styles of his native Kentucky, he borrowed blues influences from black music, the four-part harmony associated with religious singing in the South,[18] a stress on instrumental virtuosity then present in country music in general, and a tempo and rhythm stronger and faster than most country music. In the early 1940s, the instrumental composition of Monroe's group included a bass fiddle and guitar for harmonic and rhythmic accompaniment and mandolin and fiddle, which played lead or solo parts. Monroe also used an accordion for several years and either a tenor banjo or a five-string banjo (played in the frailing style) for augmented rhythmic support. The addition of Scruggs and his distinctive style of banjo playing drew enthusiastic responses from the audiences, and the banjo was given equal status with the fiddle and mandolin as a solo instrument. The standardization of the organization of Monroe's band promoted rationalization in that instruments were assigned particular roles within the ensemble. Although Monroe would briefly experiment with other additions to his band, it was the instruments and manner of performance found in his band in the mid-1940s that was soon copied by other groups (Rosenberg, 1967).

The years 1945 to 1948 are often considered the formative years of bluegrass music, and the Monroe band of that period is often mentioned with a reverence appropriate to sainthood. In this period, the music developed an ensemble sound within which improvised solo work by the instrumentalists was featured between verses of songs.[20] The popularity of the Monroe band encouraged other musicians to adopt the conventions Monroe found successful, and by the early 1950s these characteristics were being regularly referred to as bluegrass.[21] Although Monroe is today generally regarded as "father of bluegrass music," both by self-proclamation and folklorists, his commitment to a particular ensemble of instruments was not crystalized in the early fifties, and he recorded a number of songs using electric guitars, drums, and piano or organ. These recordings were not particularly successful, and Monroe's recording company soon gave up on its efforts to introduce the then-emerging "Nashville sound" into the Monroe band (Rosenberg, 1974: 46-47, 58-59).

The success of Monroe's band was overshadowed in the 1950s by the popularity of the band formed by two former members of the Blue Grass Boys, Lester Flatt and Earl Scruggs. While Monroe had wide exposure as a member of the Grand Ole Opry, the Flatt and Scruggs band, featuring Scruggs' exciting banjo playing, not only joined the Opry, but also acquired financial security. Sponsored by the Martha White Mills, the Flatt and Scruggs band had daily radio programs heard over several stations and toured extensively in the Southeast. As a consequence of this arrangement, musicians throughout the South were exposed to Scruggs' banjo style and quickly began to imitate it. A major advantage of the arrangement with the sponsor was the stability it afforded; all but one member of the band stayed with the group from 1955 through 1969. By comparison, Monroe's band was subject to extensive changes in personnel and to trying financial circumstances when the music industry changed with the appearance of rock-a-billy and the growing blend of country and "pop" music (Rooney, 1971: 71-75; Malone, 1968: 244-247). With the success of Flatt and Scruggs, however, a number of other bluegrass groups appeared in the 1950s and enjoyed limited regional success, setting the stage for the development of the next major style of banjo playing.

Melodic Style

The third major style of banjo playing is usually called melodic style. It bears a superficial similarity to the Scruggs style, but its distinctive features are sufficient for it to be recognized as a major departure. In the melodic style, the thumb and first two fingers of the right hand are used in combination with appropriate positioning of the left hand to reproduce song melodies precisely. Rather than working from right-hand rolls, as in Scruggs' style, this technique requires that each note of the melody be identified at a position on the neck of the instrument which will allow it to fit within the flow of other melody notes. In not relying on various combinations of right-hand rolls, the banjoist playing in the melodic style must predetermine the exact series of movements by the right and left hands. The melodic style offered the first opportunity to play a complete scale, a major characteristic of a truly solo instrument.[22] This accomplishment is not without its drawbacks, however; the capacity for improvisation is greatly reduced from that of the Scruggs style and the ability to perform specific tunes is greatly dependent on regular practice. And although the melodic style also produces a series of sixteenth notes, any rhythmic and harmonic characteristics are only those contained within the melody itself. This last change is particularly evident with respect to the use of the fifth string, which is struck regularly in both the frailing and Scruggs styles; while in these two styles it functions as a drone, it is only used in the melodic style in order to obtain appropriate melody notes. The expressiveness allowed by the melodic style also imposes even greater demands on the time of the banjoist; each specific melody must be worked out in a manner which will permit the achievement of a flowing melody line. In fact, a general "rule" of the melodic style is that no finger will play two consecutive notes. This style of complex (as opposed to the simple) rationality also requires that the banjoist regularly rehearse the songs in his repertoire in order to be able to play them as needed.

The melodic style was developed in the late 1950s within the context of the bluegrass band and musical form. At this time, the popularity of bluegrass music had spread from the southeastern United States to the large industrial cities of the Northeast and Midwest. In conjunction with the then-developing urban folk revival, bluegrass performers were to be found on college campuses and at folk music festivals. In comparison with some of the more "pop" oriented folk groups such as the Kingston Trio, bluegrass bands were hailed as conveyors of "authentic" folk music, and a new generation of college-educated musicians absorbed the characteristics of this musical style. About 1960, a number of banjoists, from both rural southeastern and urban northeastern backgrounds were experimenting with efforts to play old fiddle tunes in an exact, note-for-note fashion. From these attempts, the melodic style was developed.[23]

Although some examples of the melodic style were released on records intended for the urban folk music audience, it was not until Bill Keith, one of the early innovators of the style, was hired as banjoist for Bill Monroe's band, the Blue Grass Boys, that the style was widely exposed to other bluegrass musicians through Monroe's recordings and radio broadcasts. Monroe recognized the significance of Keith's style for the music that Monroe has always considered his own:

> He's [Keith] done a lot of good for music and especially for bluegrass. At a time when I needed a boost, I think that Brad [Monroe's name for Keith; there could only be one "Bill" in his band] gave it to me. I think it just came in when I needed it. Before he came along no banjo player could play those old fiddle numbers right. You have to play like Brad could play or you would be faking your way through a number. (Quoted in Rooney, 1971: 83)

The melodic style was attractive to both urban and rural listeners and performers of bluegrass music. For the urban audience, it emphasized a technical proficiency which counteracted the unsophisticated image of country music, and for the rural audience it provided new energy to old, familiar fiddle tunes. The attractiveness of the music for the urban audience is indicated by the number of non-southern musicians who followed Keith as members of Monroe's band. With backgrounds in rock, pop, folk, and classical music, young musicians from the West, Northeast, and Midwest worked for Monroe frequently in the 1960s, often leaving later to form their own bluegrass groups or work in other types of music (Rooney, 1971: 87).

In the period of the mid-1960s through the 1970s, the influx of musicians from diverse backgrounds and the influences of other forms of popular music have led to considerable experimentation in bluegrass music. While most of these experimental groups have retained the basic acoustic instrumentation of the early bluegrass band, there have been attempts to introduce electric guitars and basses, along with other instruments such as drums, piano, and steel guitar. In addition, some groups have attempted to introduce vocal styles and songs from rock, ragtime, and pop music. Among bluegrass fans and musicians, these efforts have been met with a widely divided reaction, and a distinction is often made between the "traditional" and "newgrass" groups, reflecting a clash of economic and aesthetic interests.

The newgrass bands, frequently featuring a banjo played in the melodic style, are clearly attempting to attract a wider audience, one familiar with the conventions of rock and pop music. This has alienated many who prefer "traditional, old-time" bluegrass, and most bluegrass festivals reflect this bias, banning the use of electric instruments. Bands which emphasize the music of the "golden age" of bluegrass in the 1950s rely on the pattern established by Monroe's band in the choice of material and instrumentation, using melodic-style banjo playing occasionally and generally within the context of traditional fiddle tunes.

The strong opposition to newgrass, it should be emphasized, is primarily located within the specific bluegrass audience, rather than in the general country music audience. Several long-established and generally "traditional" bluegrass groups have briefly used electric instruments but dropped them in the past few years, as bluegrass festivals have proliferated.[24] This conservative reaction, so evident among bluegrass fans, is, of course, also part of the history of country music. Despite the continual history of innovation in country music by such legendary performers as the Carter Family, Jimmy Rodgers, and others, the admonition by Grand Ole Opry founder George D. Hay to "keep it down to earth, boys" (Shelton and Goldblatt, 1966: 103), has been an ideological mainstay. This conservatism is seen in the lyrics of country music and may also be found in the continued popularity of some country performers who have not had a commercially successful record in several years. The celebration of a romanticized past, which is so strong in country music, has overcome such once-heretical innovations as the introduction of drums to the stage of the Grand Ole Opry and even the transformation of the "shrine" of country music into a Disney-style theme park.[25] In bluegrass, a similar transformation of innovation into accepted characteristics of this musical form has occurred in the case of the performance and material of the long-established (and once considered highly experimental) group from Washington, D.C., the Country Gentlemen (Malone, 1968: 329). It would seem quite likely that the current newgrass bands, if financially successful in attracting a large audience, may one day also be considered traditional.

Currently, the conservative ideology of a simpler, rural way of life is particularly evident in the bluegrass phenomenon. Supported by efforts of recording companies in the past decades to appeal to the urban folk revival audience and augmented by the urban unrest of the same period, a mystification of bluegrass music has taken place. Despite the clearly commercial origins of bluegrass, it is frequently promoted today as being "old as the hills"

(Price, 1975) and as a true folk music style. For example, writing about bluegrass, Artis states, "There is a great desire today to get back to the genuine human values, to return to the soil, to find roots in today's most common form of artistic expression — music" (1975: viii). This attraction of the pastoral ideal can only take place, as Rinzler says, "when there is an urban elite or privileged class which is separated from the idealized peasantry by education, social position and economic resources" (1976: 14). In the audiences to be found in the hundreds of bluegrass festivals held annually, this idealization of the bucolic is shared by two distinct groups: those from rural backgrounds who by virtue of occupation are now urban residents and those with urban backgrounds who seek in the music a means of rediscovering a "lost" way of life.

The Three Styles: The Structure of Musical Organization

Each of the three styles considered here developed within social and economic contexts which have resulted in the transformation of musical forms. These transformations may be examined in an analysis of the functions served by each style within the social organization of roles in the production of music. What follows is an analysis of the relationship that the frailing, Scruggs, and melodic styles have in the division of labor in music groups, specifically identifying characteristics of each style. For the purpose of analysis, a brief fragment of a tune frequently performed on the banjo provides a point of reference for the discussion.

As the accompanying figure indicates, each style produces a different version of the same tune. Although it would be necessary to provide a complete score for all instruments in a musical group to identify all of the consequences of each style, the representative measures provided here give some indication of their differences. The frailing style generally follows the melody line and contributes rhythmic and harmonic emphasis in the second measure, while the Scruggs style produces an indication of the melody line, but within arpeggios and with syncopation in the second measure. The melodic style, on the other hand, produces a flowing series of notes with minimum harmonic or rhythmic accent. Within bluegrass bands, the Scruggs and melodic styles are more compatible with the tempo of much bluegrass music and produce a more distinctive statement of the melody. Compared with the frailing style in actual ensemble performance, if not clearly evident in this example, the melodic and Scruggs styles are more dependent on other instruments for

accompaniment. Because of its rhythmic and harmonic characteristics, a banjo played in the frailing style may often be used as the
only accompaniment for a singer, but single accompaniment is virtually nonexistent in the case of the other styles. While the Scruggs
style might be used in the accompaniment of a soloist, this occurs
in conjunction with the rhythmic and harmonic support of the
bass fiddle and guitar, and with the production of harmonically
compatible arpeggios on the banjo.

FIGURE

Comparison of Three Styles of Banjo Playing

"Old Joe Clark"

The vocal part corresponding to the above examples is provided
below:

Use of the melodic style as accompaniment is infrequent, however, because of the problems created by statements of the melody on different instruments with different techniques of sound production. Finally, the repetitive movements of the frailing and Scruggs styles allow the performer to "miss" a note occasionally, while a mistake in the melodic style may cause the banjoist to miss several measures (see Wernick, 1974).

The three dominant banjo styles identified here represent historical progression toward an increased specialization of technique and a changing role of the instrument in musical ensembles. Each style may be seen within specific social contexts as a consequence of tensions arising from competing motives, to obtain expressive flexibility on the one hand and to standardize action on the other. The dominance of the frailing style in the nineteenth century owes much to its compatibility with the British-derived fiddle music in the South, the popularization and technical development of the instrument by professionals in minstrel and medicine shows, and the basic simplicity of the style itself. The appearance of the Scruggs style occurred in a period of significant growth for the country music industry, while the expanding and changing country music audience represents a response to the changes in the music itself. The rise of bluegrass music and the Scruggs style of banjo performance took place at a time in which older string bands were being replaced by more commercially successful groups, with smoother, less rustic style. Economic factors such as the financial support of radio broadcasts and the distribution of recordings promoted the widespread adoption of the Scruggs style.[26] The heightened expressiveness of this style and the fact that it increased the banjo's potential as a virtuoso instrument, elevated the banjo within the bluegrass band to the status of major importance. The melodic style owes much to the availability of bluegrass music to a mass audience, particularly as a result of the receptivity of those influenced by the urban folk revival. The melodic style followed the trend established by the Scruggs style in enhancing the capacity of the virtuoso role for the banjo, sacrificing some harmonic and rhythmic functions for the note-for-note performance of melody lines.

In the terms of Weber's description of the rationalizing effects of the professionalization of musical roles, the development of the five-string banjo and its use suggests an additional consideration. Where Weber found rationality promoted by both the conservative tendency in the use of music for magical purposes and the subsequent search for expressiveness after the music had been removed from magical contexts, the preceding discussion indicates that there may be a repetition of the process, leading to a double, or compound rationality. Weber clearly identified the rationalizing effect of the tension between standardizing and expressive interests, but did not address a condition in which professionalization may produce successive stages of rationalization. What we have seen above would indicate that the success of a particular style promotes standardization through the adoption of the style by others and that this very act of standardization establishes the conditions through which experimentation eventually results in the breaking of older stylistic rules in search of new expressive possibilities. In the case of banjo styles, the adoption of each may be seen as following this pattern as influenced by the particular economic, social, and technical factors which were present in each specific social context.

Country music has historically served to emphasize religious beliefs and the social and political conduct characteristic of its white Protestant audience, as well as expressing common concerns with employment, finances, and the social problems particularly evident in the urbanization of the South after World War II (Malone, 1968: 269-270). The celebration of traditional values which is characteristic of country music corresponds to Weber's (1958: 40) description of the function of musical forms in serving cultic or exorcistic purposes. This conservatism has supported rationalization in attempts to preserve successful musical form and simultaneously provided a basis from which experimentation could spring.

It would appear that the romanticism of the past which is so strong in country music would explain the transformation of innovations into part of a tradition-oriented mystique which obscures their recent origin. Thus, the Scruggs and melodic banjo styles are not viewed as new developments but rather as part of an unbroken history of a musical form which existed prior to the appearance of commercial country music. The styles did develop within the country music industry, however, and owe their popularity to the processes of distribution and consumption found in a mass audience. The expressive capabilities of each style, while breaking the forms set by the preceding one, have nevertheless been subsumed within the country music tradition, and the rationalization of banjo technique has followed successive steps of standardization and expressive innovation.

While each banjo style could be traced to individual ways of playing, they each gained conventionalized status as they became recognized via commercial distribution. Other personal and regional styles, both known and unrecorded, did not. This supports Rosenblum's recent assertion that stylistic conventions develop from structural and organizational features of the process of production, for both the melodic and Scruggs styles clearly emerged within commercial contexts. But the styles themselves also have an impact on the performance context in which they appear; the adoption of a particular instrumental technique within a bluegrass band, for example, alters the roles of the other instruments in various ways and changes the organization of the musical ensemble.

It would be interesting to examine the development and use of various instrumental techniques for each instrument with the bluegrass band or in other musical ensembles. A major research project would be to analyze the development of particular roles and the relationship between standardizing and expressive tendencies. Related to this would be a general investigation of the extent of the adoption of musical styles in mass audience systems of distribution. In the case of bluegrass, despite its historical ties to the country music industry in Nashville, its specific audience has always been smaller than that for other popular music forms; thus many contemporary commercial recordings are produced by small, specialized recording companies. In addition, a study of market conditions would probably contribute to a better understanding of the shaping of stylistic developments. Consistent with Weber's thesis, Rosenblum (1978) suggests that a positive relationship should exist between the level of market concentration and the standardization of styles.

Finally, in the study of the banjo styles, the romantic ideal of a simple, rural way of life provides a mystique for the specialized and interdependent nature of musical roles within the ensembles. Thus, the analysis of structural and organizational contexts of the rational development of styles should not neglect the realm of values and belief systems that support organized activity. In an age of advanced bureaucratic capitalism, the imagery so often associated with the music of the banjo serves to attract an audience from diverse geographic, educational, and occupational backgrounds by uniting them in the celebration of a lost, if not mythical, society. That, of course, is the essence of the phenomenon — a society lost to its members.

III. Social Symbolism in Joplin's Opera, *Treemonisha*

Symbolism and "False Consciousness"

A symbolic entity such as an opera does not occur in a social vacuum, but is an index to the social world which has contributed to its creation. In a limited sense, it is a form of social knowledge. However, symbolism, as opposed to more concrete knowledge, only partially expresses the society hiding behind it. As a form of knowledge, it is limited insofar as it reveals while veiling and veils while revealing; it both promotes and inhibits practical participation in the world it symbolizes (Gurvitch, 1972: 40). Opera in particular is an extremely symbolic form of expression because it is separated by a number of tacit removals from the objectivist mentality (Blasi, Dasilva, and Weigert, 1978: 323ff.; Blasi, 1977).

To fully understand a symbolic phenomenon it is necessary to place it in its societal context; such an analysis must ask why the social actor accepts as "right" or "true" a symbolic expression which is inherently and admittedly partial (Lukacs, 1971: 50). Objectively, a symbolic creation which resonates with an actor's life experiences may bring about a "false consciousness"[27] insofar as it does not directly inform the actor of the essence of his or her social circumstances; nevertheless, it is a false consciousness of a true circumstance. As such it is an improvement over a situation in which there is no consciousness at all. While one may hope for the creation of a new cultural order in which the underclasses see and understand "historical blocs" which mask their true interests, practical progress toward such a mass sociological insight must begin with the subaltern classes discovering their own personalities by means of such symbolic creations (Portelli, 1972: 142). The ultimate cultural impoverishment would be present where they do not have even that insight.

Symbolism's Social Infrastructure

> If I take . . . a theoretical statement simply as an idea, that is, "from within," I am making the same assumptions that are prescribed in it; if I take it as ideology, that is, look at it "from without," I am suspending, for a time, the whole complex of its assumptions. (Mannheim, 1971: 119)

Any intelligent interpretation which goes beyond simply naming the correlation between certain symbols and, say, social classes will certainly take the meaning of the knowledge into account, but the truth or falsity of the knowledge as determinable on its own terms must be set aside, suspended as an issue altogether. The focus must shift to the knowledge's pointing to realities beyond its direct referent, beyond itself.

Similarly, a social interpretation of a work of art goes beyond the standards or grammar of the art itself to the social realities which it both reveals and veils. Lucien Goldmann approached exceptional works of art as embodiments of world views; he then set about looking for the social background reality behind the world view in question (e.g., Goldmann, 1964: see Goldmann, 1969: 102). In his view, it was a historical fact that these background realities have been social classes since ancient times, but he did not propose that this should always be the case. In the discussion that follows, it will be shown that racial and ethnic groups can also be relevant factors within a larger class structure.

It remains to be seen how the social researcher is to decide what given works of art symbolically or indirectly express. Goldmann proposed that such works exist as virtual collective consciousness to the extent that what they express is not peculiar to the author but shared by the others in the social group (Goldmann, 1969: 129). Although this might seem arbitrary, it is obviously necessary to see the artistic creator for what he is sociologically in order to develop an adequate interpretation of his work. The social location of the creative artist is therefore a key datum; it is obviously a clearer datum in some cases than in others.

The Sociological Potential of Symbolism

In his analysis of the culture of southern Italy, Gramsci noted that the southern intellectual (white-collar worker) provided a cultural linkage which tied the lower classes to the aristocracy. The serious culture, to the extent that the peasantry partook of it, made the peasant a subordinate participant in another class's cultural expressions, thereby forestalling any independent cultural expression on the part of the peasant class. This constituted the "monstrous agrarian bloc" which enabled the southern middle class to act as an agent of both northern capital and southern landownership (Gramsci, 1975: 45). If the southern peasant were provided the wherewithal to evolve an independent symbolic expression, the "monstrous agrarian bloc" would be undermined, and this could lead to a class discovering its own personality, its own potential for efficacious action. Here we will look at Scott Joplin's *Treemonisha* as an independent cultural expression of an underclass in the United States.

Joplin's Treemonisha

The Composer's Life Experiences and the "Talented Tenth"

Scott Joplin was born in 1868 to a working-class family in the town of Texarkana. His father, a railroad laborer, was an ex-slave from North Carolina, his mother a black from Kentucky. The elder Joplin, his wife and his other sons had all at one time or another earned extra money as musicians. Scott became fascinated with the piano and showed considerable talent at it. A local music teacher, a German immigrant whose name has been lost to history, was so impressed with Scott that he gave him free lessons in piano performance and harmony. He also aroused Joplin's interest in serious music by playing works of the great composers. Joplin never forgot his benefactor and in later years, when the old man was ill and poor, he sent him gifts of money (Gammond, 1975: 29).

Joplin left home at the age of fourteen and became a wandering honky-tonk pianist. His mother had recently died, and he had quarreled with his father, who wanted him to work at a steady job rather than lead the marginal existence of a Negro entertainer. He traveled through much of the Mississippi basin, earning meager wages and tips in various seamy establishments, but eventually gained a local reputation in St. Louis and Sedalia, Missouri. Once he was able to settle down somewhat in Sedalia, he studied harmony and composition in the Smith School of Music, a department of the George R. Smith College for colored people. During that time he composed music for a male vocal octet on a regular basis (Gammond, 1975: 60).

Joplin began to compose syncopated music with jagged melodies, as a serious undertaking, but he was unable to find a publisher for these works. What he was able to publish was unremarkable pseudo-white music. Eventually, the publisher John Stark of Sedalia (later of St. Louis) discovered him when he was playing the now famous "Maple Leaf Rag" in the Maple Leaf Club in Sedalia. Stark published the work and many other Joplin "rags." The publisher turned down a ragtime ballet, however, and he refused to consider a ragtime opera, *A Guest of Honor,* which has since been lost.

After his marriage ended in divorce, Joplin moved first to Chicago and then New York. He spent considerable effort collaborating on compositions with other, lesser-known black composers in order to help them out. "One of Joplin's best remembered traits was that he was always ready to help a fellow composer and never uttered a word of jealousy or condemnation" (Gammond, 1975: 61). He is described as a modest and retiring man and an accomplished though not a virtuoso performer. His ambition was to be a composer of serious music; indeed, he disliked the term *ragtime* as a name for his best known genre of work. However, he never gained acceptance among the black musicians of New York; they associated him with the "low-class" rag music and avoided such provincial styles (Gammond, 1975: 27, 22, 83).

Joplin married again in 1909, and perhaps could have had a comfortable life in New York if it were not for his ambition. His wife ran the building they owned as a theatrical boardinghouse, and he used it as a ragtime conservatory, composing many new pieces there as well. However, he devoted increasing amounts of time and most of his money to a new opera, *Treemonisha.* With the support of his wife, who believed in the work, he abandoned his other concerns. He failed to interest anyone else in the project, however, and succeeded only in winning a laudatory review of the vocal score in the June 24, 1911 issue of *American Musician* (Jones, 1975: 13; Gammond, 1975: 98). Most reaction was simply incredulous.

Although he was nearing the end of his resources, Joplin rented a hall in Harlem and in 1915 led a cast of vocalists through a trial performance, playing the piano himself. He was hoping to attract backers for a full production, but without an orchestra, the opera was thin and unconvincing. He was crushed, and the failure of the work is assumed to have hastened his premature death.

Joplin's opera failed because of prejudice on the part of whites and a failure of nerve on the part of blacks; his project was simply unthinkable in his time. The limited gains made by the American black during the Civil War and the Reconstruction time were at a standstill. W. E. B. DuBois was calling upon his fellow prosperous blacks to improve the lot of the whole black community (DuBois, 1967 [1899]: 316-317), but the efforts of the "talented tenth"[28] of the black population had not yet borne fruit, and black achievements were not given the attention they deserved. A black with too much talent and ambition was likely to face more grief than success.

Treemonisha: *Opera as Allegory of Joplin's World*

The setting of *Treemonisha* is rural Arkansas, September 1884, near Joplin's childhood home. The story is a simple one: Local blacks decline to buy charms from a conjuror after an educated eighteen-year-old girl, Treemonisha, discourages them. As a group is husking corn after a square dance, Treemonisha begins to collect leaves from an old tree for a wreath. Monisha, her assumed mother, tells her not to disturb the tree, for she first found Treemonisha under that tree as an infant. She and her husband have raised Treemonisha as their own, seeing to it that a white lady (a parallel to Joplin's German music teacher) taught her to read and write. Treemonisha and a friend leave the scene and later the friend returns to report that the conjuror and his cohorts have kidnapped Treemonisha. While the conjurors plot to push their captive into a wasps' nest, Remus, who has been taught by Treemonisha and now despises superstition, shows up dressed in an outrageous scarecrow costume. The conjurors flee, thinking he is the devil. As Treemonisha is returning home with Remus, they pass a group working in a field; naturally the group sings some work songs. At home, Treemonisha dissuades the people from punishing the conjurors, who have been captured by Treemonisha's friends. The conjurors promise to abandon their Voodoo superstition, while the people choose Treemonisha as their leader. They dance in celebration.

The opera strikes the hearer as a mixture of ethnic, small town, and establishment musical styles. Monisha's story, "The Sacred Tree," is a lilting ballad. The work crew encountered en route home sings a barbershop quartet. There is some ragtime, most notably the concluding dance, "A Real Slow Drag," which is strong and stately. There are also choral/orchestral ensembles and a rolling basso aria. Treemonisha and Remus speak in standard English, while the other characters use black dialect. Thus the very musical styles and linguistic patterns bring the rural black ways and the black mastery of the white ways onto the same stage. Significantly, the ethnically black music and the small town America music are as dignified as the ethnically white music of the metropolis. Musically, the work is not a ragtime opera, but an opera of multiple styles.

The shape of black hopes is pointed out directly. Education will dispel the ignorance which holds the black people down. Black forgiving black and leaving the way open for other blacks' improvement is a theme which appears in the climax of the plot. There is an eloquent silence with respect to the role of the white. However, there are other layers of communication in the opera which go beyond these obvious themes.

Moving from the message of the story to indirect reflection of the larger society, one cannot miss Joplin's nostalgia for the societal periphery. As with many rural-to-urban migrants, he was able to bring forth picturesque scenes out of his childhood. The black and small town flavor of much of the music strengthens the vividness of this reminiscence (see Dasilva and Faught, 1978). In this quality it is somewhat similar to such operas as *Cavalleria Rusticana* and *L'Elisir d'Amore*. The work also portrays the caste mentality of the black community: the black conjurors oppose the advancement represented by Treemonisha's education.[29] This reflective level of communication operates through the tacit assumptions which are shared by Joplin and his intended audience.

Even more intriguing is the socially structured psychology allegorized in the opera; the allegory represents a third level of communication. The world was not yet ready for the talented tenth, not yet ready for someone like Joplin.[30] The black and white communities' resistance to Joplin's own entry into serious music is recapitulated in the libretto under the form of a kidnapping; as Treemonisha was held captive amid the voodooism of the conjurors, Joplin was held captive in the musical equivalent thereof during his years as a wandering honky-tonk performer. His psychological adjustment to the dashing of his artistic hopes took, evidently, the form of forgiveness — the reverse side, as it were, of Joplin's own self-destruction. One cannot help but sense the genuineness of the appeals for punishment in the opera's last act, but these appeals in the end give way to forgiveness. This mentality seems to presage the often heard appeals of black leaders after the assassination of Martin Luther King, Jr., to the effect that King himself would not have wanted any retaliatory violence.

The Message Which Evoked Resistance

The black musicians of New York who rejected Joplin's serious treatment of black and folklike music undoubtedly had ambitions for themselves, but they did not sense the plausibility of the revolutionary ambition hinted at in *Treemonisha*. A revolution (as opposed to a rebellion) which accorded high status to an expression of black and rural culture was still beyond the cognitive grasp of the turn-of-the-century mind.

To desire a better life was only the first step out of a caste mentality. W. E. B. DuBois had already made the class analyses which provided black leadership with the basis of a collective strategem, and from 1910 onward his influence was evident. However, the abstractions of legal equality and the individualism entailed in educational and economic improvement did not give the collective black identity full status. This could only be achieved through the symbolic realm in which the medium is a major part of the message; the identifiably black medium must itself find status before its message can be taken at face value. Surely *Treemonisha* was ahead of its time, but it was premature symbolically rather than intellectually. Its intellectual message — that education held out hope for black people — had already gained acceptance and had been articulated by Booker T. Washington. Indeed, such faith in education is part of what gives the libretto a quaint, rural aspect.

Conclusion

It was noted above that in neo-Marxist thought social classes and other significant categories are thought to discover their personalities in the symbolic realm and then to articulate their interests in a more prosaic manner (see also Maduro, 1976: 176). The fact that *Treemonisha* failed, however, after black thinkers' prosaic analyses had become more than adequate suggests a different sequence. It seems that once black thinkers had sufficiently focused on the problems of American blacks, what was needed was a less intellectual communication for the nonpolitically oriented and the nonphilosophers. These latter categories of people were not prepared for *Treemonisha,* and the black intellectuals had not been looking to the fine arts as a medium for their ideas.

Considering that it was not until 1955 that Martin Luther King's Christian, nonviolent movement inspired confidence among black people, one could conclude that Joplin was about forty years ahead of his time. By 1955, black and rural music had been assimilated by whites to such an extent that it was no longer either ethnically black nor geographically peripheral. The multileveled message of cultural equality assumed instead a theological-hortatory form in which white legitimacy could be subjected to a critique on equal terms. Black theology and religious forms served where black music could no longer do so.

There is a certain irony in this. The hardheaded critique which consigns the symbolic universes of discourse (for example, opera and religion) to insignificance with such loaded terms as *false consciousness* and *mystification* depends upon such symbolic realms for its own social efficacy. The critique itself becomes a material force only after it has "gripped the masses" (see Marx, 1967: 257) through symbolism.

Finally, the example of Joplin's multilevel communication suggests the role of the artist in class dynamics. Following Goldmann, every class or category of individuals is a "trans-individual subject." Its world view is held in common, and even a world view which it finds tempting but which it is not ready to accept is sensed as such collectively. Only a few members of the social collectivity express in their own individual consciousnesses the full world view or vision in question. "Certain 'exceptional men' are able to give expression to this total experience, and produce the world-vision as a whole" (Lovell, 1973: 308). The artist is the person who articulates the multileveled aspects of the collective world view through the multiple levels inherent in artistic expression.

IV. The Social Content of the *Prole do Bebê* of Heitor Villa-Lobos

International Context

The end of World War I marked the conclusion of the first stage of capitalism, that of colonialism (Candido, 1973; Fernandes, 1973). From then on relations between the European metropolitan centers and the quasi-colonial periphery evolved to an increasing emphasis on nativism and nationalism in the colonized or periphery countries. These developments are particularly characteristic of transformations in high culture. While German, French, and Italian cultural dominance represented a rationalism and individualism that was to achieve a universality of thought and style by transcending national origins, on the periphery there was a sustained concentration on forms and themes which expressed "national character" (Andrade, 1936). In this context the "universality" of the European traditions clashed with the "will to survive" in the peripheral nations. Although the European nations maintained a continuing material dominance, with European thought benefitting from the resultant traditional legitimacy and the weight of organizational complexity, the divisive bid for hegemony in Europe in the 1914–1918 conflict weakened European control over the colonies (both political colonies and economic hinterlands) and presented the periphery peoples an opportunity to formulate their national individualities (Adorno, 1955 and 1973). In effect the fragmentation of European culture created crevices and models to be adopted, without hegemony, by the periphery, for as the European nations broke away from one another culturally, each seizing upon a fragment or two in order to build anew, the peripheral nations could also seize upon their own modes of cultural differentiation.

Musical Context

With the rise of colonial nationalism, there was a multiplication of movements advocating a change in various art forms, certainly including music. Little innovation had previously appeared especially in music composition. Then came a new mood which justified and extended the music innovation which had developed in Europe in the two decades before 1914. A new musical phase was very much in evidence.

What characterized this new phase? Romanticism was the harmonic phase par excellence. The richness and harmonic complexity of the works of Wagner, Frank, Strauss, and Debussy brought about the destruction of traditional harmony (Adorno, 1963 and 1973). Harmony based on tonality is broken when C major loses its central position of order and power. The uses in romanticism of Asiatic and North African modes, as well as deficient and whole sound scales, were counterposed to the requirements of traditional harmony, contributing to its breakdown. For instance, the rules for chord construction through the superimposition of thirds were superseded with the proliferation of constructs on the bases of fourths, fifths, and seconds. Whereas Debussy often operated with scales of whole sounds and

Schönberg systematically constructed harmony through super-posed fourths and the atonal scale, in Brazil, for instance, research on national roots disclosed the dominant use of the hipofrigian and hipolidian scales in indigenous music (Andrade, 1936).

Not only did harmony change radically, but spinning off from romanticism, composers became much more individualistic in their notation systems, so that writing, as well as instrumenta-tion (including "modified" instruments) and directions often changed from composer to composer.[31]

With romantic harmony exhausting the potential of chords and modulations (as in works at the beginning of the century by Debussy, Ravel, Strauss, and Scriabin), harmony virtually broke down (Greisman, 1976). The moderns, in order to develop new ways, directed their work toward atonality and polytonality (both already appearing in romanticism). Atonality was first fully de-veloped by Arnold Schoenberg in 1908.[32] It was based on the twelve-tone scale with consecutive intervals of half sounds: the chromatic scale (Adorno, 1973). Atonality, thus, did not recognize the existence of tonality. On the other hand, polytonality, as developed particularly in France (Igor Stravinsky, etc.), used simultaneous tonalities in addition to the sounds of harmony, rhythms, and polyphony. Beyond these solutions, a third, named "fugitive tonality," also appeared, a process which, according to Hindemith, without systematically escaping the tonal sense and without modulating according to the principles of harmony, used changes in the significant degrees of tonality (fourth, fifth, and even first). What occurred was a continuous tonal evasion, bringing about a complete rupture of the classical concept of modulation, which called for the passage from one fixed tonality to another.

The focus on the dynamic value of intervals replacing the categories of consonance and dissonance established a new concept of sound equilibrium. Such changes in harmony also affected the concept and use of melody, polarized between the use of popular materials and quasi subordination to harmonic construction (for example, the brutalization of voice and the incorporation of all variants of non-singing voice in Strauss's *Electra*). The song, often incorporated into the cantata, led to a decrease in the interest in the melodic part and shifted the attention to the whole of the composition.[33] Vocal effects multiply, changing the character of "bel canto"[34] or shifting to micro pieces.[35] The importance of rhythm was also extended and its measures were multiplied to a complex polyrhythm. Emphasis was no longer on the combination of rhythms, but rather on the sound movement of the whole composition.[36]

Villa-Lobos

These changes should be viewed within the context of certain of Villa-Lobos' biographical experiences. Heitor Villa-Lobos was born in Rio de Janeiro, March 5, 1890. His father, Raul Villa-Lobos, was dedicated to the arts and was himself a cellist. By the age of twelve, Villa-Lobos was already making successful public appearances with the cello. Despite the personal hardships that befell his family with the death of his father, the support of his mother enabled him to continue his studies under some of the best teachers in Rio. Particularly notable in this respect were Angelo França and Francisco Braga. At nineteen Villa-Lobos began to give cello concerts and play in orchestras. By 1915, he began to show his compositions, and as early as 1920 he was discussed as a significant composer.[37]

In 1918 he had met Artur Rubenstein, who, among others, encouraged him to further his studies in Europe. Rubenstein, in fact, added some of the young man's compositions to his repertoire and brought them to the attention of a French publisher. Thus, by the late 1920s, Villa-Lobos' music was arousing violent controversy in the major centers of music. He was recognized as the outstanding new force dominating Brazilian music and became the best known of all Latin American composers (Bettencourt, 1945).

It is possible to enumerate the influences apparent at different stages in his career: in chronological sequence, Wagner and Puccini; then Debussy as revealed to him by Rubenstein in 1918; Milhaud and Ravel during his stays in Paris in the 1920s; Bela Bartok, who responded warmly to him; and finally Bach (Bettencourt, 1945). Moreover, he incorporated melodies, harmonies, rhythms, and "moods" from the Brazilian musical background of Indian, African, and Portuguese sources, as well as cultural influences derived from Spain, France, and Italy. He produced upwards of 2,500 works, encompassing all known forms and a few of his own invention, from *Choros* with its origins in the work of Stravinsky, to impressionistic piano pieces, ballets, symphonies, quartets, songs, oddities such as music from a graph of the New York skyline, choruses for forty thousand voices, and the "Bachianas" series in a neoclassical style that recalled both Bach and Bacchus.

Prole do Bebê

Prole do Bebê (The Baby's Children) was composed in 1918 and stands as a charming and imaginative suite of eight pieces based on traditional children's tunes, reflecting the influence of French impressionistic traditions. Each short piece (the entire suite lasts a little more than fifteen minutes) is named for a different doll that evokes aspects of the exotic racial and social content of Brazilian life (Vassberg, 1969). The *Prole do Bebê* includes the following: "Branquinha" (Little White Porcelain Doll), "Moreninha" (Little Dark Papier-mâché Doll), "Caboclinha" (Little *Cabocla* Terra-cotta Doll), "Mulatinha" (Little Mulatta Rubber Doll), "Negrinha" (Little Negress Wooden Doll), "A Pobrezinha (Little Beggar Rag Doll), "O Polichinelo" (Punch), and "A Bruxa" (Witch Cloth Doll).

The Whole and Its Parts

The suite is an old type of composition made up of several parts.[38] The earliest organizing principle of the suite was derived from dance and was structured as a totality through the addition and opposition of four characteristic dance types: allemande, courante, sarabande, and gigue.[39] These were most often introduced by a prelude. In the nineteenth century, with the extension of romanticism, the suite often took on orchestral form, becoming a kind of symphonic fantastic divertissement and losing its traditional characteristic rules.

In its classical version the suite integrated concern with "pure music" (characteristic of the composer as a specialist worker) with the social context by adding the operation of compositional rules (harmony) to the social referent of dance, well known to the public. The alternation of the various types of dance helped give a certain dynamic equilibrium to the whole suite.[40] Thus, in the classical suite we would find the following sequence:

allemande: animated allegretto in two beats

courante: slow and grave, three beats with two choruses repeated twice sarabande: slow and grave, slow rhythm in three beats

gigue: rapid and light, two beats in a 6/8 measure

Consequently the totality would make up the structure: active-determined, slow-meditative, slow-resoluted, and active-liberative. Whereas the first part would function to attract the audience's attention, the two middle sections would allow instrumental elaboration, and the last would conclude the piece with animation and gaiety, thus underscoring the work of the musician vis-à-vis the audience. Moreover, the appeal to known rhythms would facilitate the interaction between musician and public, allowing the latter to bring in its own musical concerns in the middle sections.

As romanticism moved beyond its creative potential, these classical bases of the suite were broken, and the mediation between audience and musician was often made through pictorial, literary, or nostalgic descriptions (such as in the use of folk and popular themes), rather than through the use of known dance forms (Greisman, 1976). The structural devices used for a harmonic totality in the classical period came to be replaced with multiple centers of interest emphasized by complexities of harmonic construction and technical displays of performance.

In Villa-Lobos' *The Baby's Children,* the situation is evident. Beginning with the linguistic names given for the pieces ("Branquinha," "Moreninha," etc.) and concluding with the name of the whole suite, one finds heterogeneity and inconsistency. Certainly a baby cannot really have children unless it is a mythical baby (e.g., the nation Brazil) or the use is metaphorical (the children are not really children but dolls).

Both meanings are present in the composition and in its general frame of "children's music" (Wenz, 1929). Brazil has often been considered a young country, its existing problems of development reflecting growing pains of adolescence. Certainly, these notions are ideological, since the country was discovered and first settled in the sixteenth century. Other American nations are similarly "young" but not as underdeveloped. The young-old metaphor exemplifies the supranational global structure of domination and dependence in the economic and cultural spheres. The relationship may be further extended to include "parents" (metropolitan centers), baby (the dependent nation), and its children/dolls (its dependent members) — thus unveiling not only a structural network relating center to periphery, but also a structural formation of hierarchy and domination within the periphery. The underlying political implications of this construct are veiled under the metaphor of a musical suite self-classified as "children's music," which minimizes the rudeness of self-exposure and yet allows the cryptic message to be presented, heard, and received. Certainly, this is an ambiguous message, but still one which can convey its disguised, potentially critical character.

Furthermore, in such a casting there is another dimension that identifies the absent composer. The musical object is expressive of the interacting dynamics of the composer and the national reality. In the looking glass, Villa-Lobos sees himself (the Brazilian, looking at Brazil as a Brazilian) still as exotic, as one looking from the center would see the periphery. To note a parallel case, this is the position from which Darius Milhaud also composed works such as *Saudades do Brasil: Tijuca, Corcovado,* and the suite *Boeuf sur le Toit.* The real position of the composer is a transitive one. From the metropolitan center he, being a Brazilian composer, is the exotic one; from his own position of creator, looking at his country, the country is exotic. While maintaining that position, he also views the dolls from an outside viewpoint, that of the male composer, and again all are "exotic."

The signs that identify the sequence of pieces in the suite are also not determinant of a homogeneous universe, thereby underscoring the heterogeneity of the pictured universe of the author (the country). Among Baby's children are three categories: (1) young females: representing all the major ethnic types in the country — white, dark, caboclo, mulatto, black; (2) two ostensive socioeconomic groups: again caboclo, and beggar; and (3) an extraneous category which includes nonconformists: one young male (Punch) and one female (witch). The descriptive materiality of the dolls identifies their differential social importance. The single exception is the character Punch, a male character, twice removed from the category of baby's children (1) by being a male and thus less in a position of subordination, and (2) by being Punch, thus under the sign of an active character that plays havoc with situations. All the other dolls (even the witch, who despite being a woman is distinguished by her old age and her ability to act magically upon reality) are socially and economically differentiated by their stated materiality and the status of their constitutive materials: porcelain, papier-mâché, terra-cotta, rubber, wood, rags, and cloth. The superior substance is also linked with the superior social stratum (e.g., procelain-white).

Socially, the main population groups of Brazil are present:

white (European, made of porcelain, the best identified with
Sèvres), black (African, made of wood, identified with—in Brazil—
roughness and primitivism), and their mixture, mulatto ("local,"
made of rubber, a native product of Brazil). There is no Amerindian
doll, which by its absence expresses the slight numerical and social
significance of Amerindians in coastal Brazil. Nonetheless, the
mixture of white and Amerindian is present in the cabocla doll.
The terra-cotta cabocla doll immediately recalls a label of socio-
ethnic classification peculiar to Brazil, i.e., the *branco-da-terra* (lit-
erally "earth-white"). With respect to color, this category socially
classifies those with whitish skin, although a "white" not equivalent to the prominent white European group. There are additional
negative implications of backwardness, provincialism, isolationism, rudeness, and cunning. *Moreninha* (in the usual English trans-
lation, "dark") denotes, at the time that Villa-Lobos wrote the
composition, a southern European type rather than a dark negroid
type. It clearly emphasizes a difference, both ethnic and qualitative, between northern and southern European groups and the
opposition between their given materiality. In this respect porcelain
and papier-mâché underscore qualitative differences.

As a whole, then, all the pieces are either signs of dependence
(women in patriarchal society), marginals (Punch and old witch),
or all exotic, especially in their quaint foreign character, which is
not to be taken seriously in the "really" important and significant
affairs of the world of powerful men or metropolitans, since they
are all playing their childish games in baby's family (see Ricoeur,
1973). Still, under this facade they make their point, and in fact
reflect the country's tensions beneath the mask of expected and
harmless differences. The triad composed of the Little Beggar Doll,
Punch, and the Witch Cloth Doll portrays tensions that are less
likely to disappear in the catharsis of their social roles. This points
up Villa-Lobos' insight regarding the dynamic potential of poverty,
maverick males, and cunning older women playing havoc with the
existing internal order of affairs. Still, it is a game, being played
within the dependent society, within its intertwined structure of
internal dependence. It contrasts with any "game" within the
center-periphery structure. There are no mythical heroes of liberation: Villa-Lobos does not even appropriate the heroes of Brazilian
traditions, such as Dom Sabastiao (who emerges in many of the
messianic folk movements), Canudos, Condestado, and so on.

The Musical Material and Its Utilization

The composition dates from 1918, a time when Villa-Lobos met Artur Rubenstein and when he was influenced by the works of Debussy. The mode of composition is certainly marked by the technical operation of impressionism, similar to Debussy's (Wenk, 1976). Debussy had used the suite form, with "mood pieces" rather than pictorial idealizations.[41] The frame of a child's suite had certainly been used before Villa-Lobos took it up, most importantly by J. S. Bach, with the *Book of Ann Magdalene Bach* during the "classic" period and by Robert Schumann in his *Scenes from Childhood,* Opus 15, in the romantic period (besides many others).[42]

In Villa-Lobos' case the childhood theme seems quite ambiguous (Schwartz, 1967). The suite is very demanding technically, indicating the virtuoso character given to the piece by the composer. It was not intended for children's training (as in the case of Bach), nor for reminiscences of childhood which are pure even in their technical simplicity (as in Schumann). The suite contains elements of self-reflection (as in Debussy's), but at a distance, since all the pieces reflect girl's themes, except Punch, and in this case the image of a maverick who resembles Villa-Lobos, who himself played such a role in the world of music, especially in Brazil. As in Ravel's children's work, it has a quasi-noble element, particularly notable in "Caboclinha" and "Pobrezinha"; in both cases, a sorrowfulness underlines the hopeless status of these groups in the emerging competitive world of modernizing Brazil.

Let us note some of the specific attributes of each piece in the suite. The "Little White Doll" is composed as a "modinha" (a kind of lieder), circular and questioning. In an allegro vivo it recalls the *Valse Mystique* (Rio, 1917), brilliant, always legato, with a circular organization. Rather than the pure, carefree woman imagined to exist in the ballrooms of Austria or France, there is an admixture of idealized romantic ethereality characteristic of much nineteenth-century literature, where pale languishing heroines are often portrayed as slowly dying of tuberculosis (Sontag, 1978). Throughout the pieces of the first segment of the suite (nos. 1-5), the composition remains, nevertheless, most assertive and generally progressive, resembling the romantic notion of tuberculosis in which the victim is seen as undergoing contrasting moments:

"white pallor and red flush, vitality alternating with languidness" (Sontag, 1978: 11). The melodic theme immediately triggers reminiscences of an Austrian waltz. Playing the higher octaves with the right hand recalls a music box and a sort of carefree attitude, while remaining superficial, as would be appropriate for an upper-class woman in the nineteenth century.

The "Little Dark Papier-mâché Doll" is written as an animato, with the rapid execution of a theme by the right hand repeated as an alternating voice by the left hand. The accompaniment is rodante, and the affirmative theme ends in a question. The quasi happy left hand introduces an ancient melancholy despite the sparkling freshness of the right hand. Chromatic variations with a rodante form underline the symbolic gaiety attributed by the culture to the "moreninha." This ethnic group is expressive of the Mediterranean area, which received much Arabic influence, especially in southern Portugal and Spain. The transfer of this element to Brazil made it an important component of the population. But, in most cultural works the type remains constructed externally, since up to the time of this composition very little research (besides that of Arthur Ramos in anthropology) was available. In music the pioneer work in ethnomusicology and folklore conducted by Mario de Andrade (1936, 1938, 1940) has focused on the imperial era "modinhas" and expanded into caboclo and Amerindian materials. Thus, the Portuguese folk materials used in this composition remain sketchy and appear but briefly in the emerging ciranda.

The "Little Cabocla Terra-cotta Doll" thematically portrays the distant "empty territory" through a slow and nostalgic tempo (Dasilva and Faught, 1978). As elsewhere, the melody is fused with the rhythmic structure played by the left hand.[43] Rhythm and melody are concentrated in the left hand, whereas the significant role of the right hand is confined to the repetition of notes with an accent effect. The syncopated rhythm of the left hand in the lower keyboard, with the addition of an intertwined sequence and the accents of the higher keyboard, support the feeling of sadness and the mood of distance and nostalgia. These are stereotypical attributes imputed to the caboclo by the urban populations, supported by the isolative character of the caboclo adaptation to the land, where the archaic elements are, in fact, quite functional (Candido, 1964).

The "Little Mulatta Rubber Doll" is constructed as a prelude with the alternation of low and high chords linked through ornamental scales in the form of an andante. The variation of tempo from allegrissimo to scherzo produces the impression of a fountain of sounds in the higher register which contrasts with the cutting points in the lower keyboard. Such contrasts portray tensions and conflicts; the solution in the higher keyboard is tempered with a coda to a sequence which has a nostalgic character, ending in a quasi martial yet somber mood. Such a construction is quite congruent with stereotypes of the mulatto group in Brazil and even throughout the Atlantic coast of Latin America, and is probably best characterized with the poetic line that describes the mulatto as the "sad being, a product of two sad races" (viz., Portuguese and African). At the same time, these stereotypes attribute to the mulatto a gaiety and carefree attitude toward life.[44] These stereotypical inconsistencies are thus reflected in the musical reconstruction advanced in the work by Villa-Lobos (Schwartz, 1970).

The "Little Negress Wooden Doll" is a composition in tempo vivace using staccato execution with sforzando accents. It is quite rapid, with a moto perpetuo effect in the higher keyboard and accents in the lower keyboard. The second part introduces a ciranda theme, and the composition ends with a question. Phrases of irregular length contribute to an unsettling effect of the music despite its tempo and undulating structure. Excluding the title, little real material of African origin enters this composition. This contrasts with the richness of the African contribution to Brazilian music.[45] What emerges is more of a *ciranda* type (a children's circular dance). It imitates a black musical form but one which is already incorporated into the mixed urban society and is thereby diluted. It is more of a paternalistic expression than an affirmative portrayal of the black presence in its own right in the country (see Marcuse, 1972).

The "Little Beggar Rag Doll" is a transitional piece in the total structure of the suite. It both separates and links the five "little women" of the first part and the two characters of the last part. The composition is written in moderato and muito dolente, with a rubato tempo, a situation already found in the caboclo piece. The mood is again nostalgic and sad, with an expression of a certain fatalistic attitude. These similarities are homologous with the structural position of the caboclo in the society as a whole (in the urban-rural axis, for instance, the caboclo occupies the differentiated position of poverty, archaism, and isolation) and that of the "poor," the underclass in urban society (often a product of rural-to-urban migration, also isolated from the mainstream of life through economic and social deprivation). Moreover, this is the poor of Rio around the twenties — deprived and beaten — and is quite distinct from the poor of the favelas of the sixties who entered revolutionary music and the theater of liberation, fighting for their rights, if not affirming their significance.[46]

The suite ends with the "Witch Cloth Doll" and "Punch." The first is written as a vivo parallel to another Villa-Lobos composition, the *Rodante* (No. 3 of *Simples Colentânea*, Rio, 1919). It develops in the upper keyboard in a brilliant cirandinha, expressive but not clear melodically; in an undulating movement the cirandinha reappears with accents by the left hand and ends with a veloce into glissando. "Punch" is a brilliant and gay piece in a scherzo form; this is followed by a dramatic section, with a questioning left hand slowing into a sad singing that alternates with a questioning answer by the left hand and ends with a question. Both compositions are show pieces of technical skill for the performer, playing the role that ending pieces did in the classical suite by breaking up in high-spirited play the formality of the relationships between performer and audience, and giving the performer the upper hand.

The Reconstitution of the Whole

If we view Villa-Lobos' suite in light of the process of transformation of structures, it is difficult to see how the suite develops except in terms of Gurvitch's complex dialetic (1962; see Blasi, Dasilva, and Weigert, 1978). Starting with the suite form in its most abstract and formal aspects, in this case the form is translated into multiple racial (ethnic) polarities. The polarities are followed by a synthesis in the transitional moment of the suite exemplifying poverty and the suite concludes with the apparition of the witch and Punch. Thus, the real, lived, experiential existence of the country, already muted through the simulated focus of a child's lenses, is now, after passing through the unnamed majority of the Brazilian population (referred to by the various dolls), "solved" through two possible solutions: that is, through magic, or the braggadocio of Punch, the irreverent grown-up child who plays dirty and flaunts the rules. While a maverick and carefree actor, Punch is still just an actor.

But we can go beyond this level of analysis. We can recall the contrasting socioeconomic and cultural dimensions of national states such as Brazil and the United States. On the extreme, one could posit the question of the conflicts illustrated by the suite in terms of scarcity and elitism. The structures available are, politically and economically, radically different. Whereas someone like John Cage (see Middleton, 1972) can be read and listened to by generations of students attending colleges and schools in the United States and elsewhere, those who heard Villa-Lobos in a country like Brazil (with a population already of millions) could be counted in the thousands, at best. The dominated character of Brazilian culture did not allow the attempt at communication, let alone "undistorted communication" in Habermas's sense, that one can find elsewhere.

Regarding the dialectical resolution presented by Villa-Lobos in the suite, a possible hypothesis is that he was taking the "best" available solution for a creator-male in the developing society of urban Rio, then being exposed to metropolitan ways through Rubenstein and others. Further, if the influences of the first period of Villa-Lobos career were not shaken by the dominating new metropolitan trends, possibly the whole composition would have ended up in a much more Italianated result, of unabashed romanticism. But what we really have is a childish play of a Punch, or the return to roots through a periodical magic dimension. Both are "unmodern" ways to deal with realities, and in the context of urban Rio, both are "flights of the mind," escapist possibilities, tenable only through the remarkable "fireworks" of technical skills given to the pianist in his bag of tricks as a seller of a commodity for a society that is moved by the "oddities of performers" (as in the old-time sideshows), or by the pseudo-exoticism of a music coming from the periphery of the "empire."

If one inquires into the musical construction, one notes the pervasive character of a "nostalgia-sadness" that stands in contradiction to the "carefree-happiness" moods. These states are always linked through modulations, arpegios, chromatic scales, or other variants of elaboration. Such a construction illustrates a duality of character and the ambivalence of these two "ways of existing" in the national character (Burman, Dasilva, et al., 1975). Considered in this light, the themes of the suite are even further extended: the metropolis-colony axis becomes clearer, and the dialectical solution given by Villa-Lobos is the one expected and established in the metropolis. The resolution presented is that of carefree slaves, happy-go-lucky beings, intertwining joking behavior and alienation, with a few drops of a magic spell for help.

Appendix

Most of the research techniques used in sociology for the study of social phenomena are entirely appropriate for the sociological study of music. A number of texts and manuals which cover such techniques as interviewing, survey research, participant observation, unobtrusive methods, and other forms of quantitative and qualitative inquiry can be readily adapted to the interest of the sociologist studying musical conduct. These techniques can be found in a variety of sources, and a complete review of them here would take far too much space. Measurements of social class standing, attitude surveys, analysis of interactional events, phenomenological analysis, and other procedures can be applied directly to the study of individuals involved in music-related activity, whether the focus is on the characteristics of participants; attitudes toward music, musicians, and audiences; interaction among musicians or between musicians and others; or music experiences. None of these techniques, of course, can replace a mastery of sociological concepts and the use of these concepts in acquiring an understanding of the contexts in which musical conduct occurs.

Since a principal assumption in the sociology of music is that social processes themselves influence the very nature of the music, it is of major importance for sociologists to attend to musical characteristics themselves. The need to analyze music is difficult to satisfy, for most individuals do not have the necessary background in both sociology and music. While this deficiency could be remedied by the sociologist collaborating with a musicologist, this solution is not always possible for a variety of reasons; the sociologist must then turn to other approaches. This appendix will review some techniques which are especially appropriate. The student can learn of many other techniques by reading the various research articles which are listed in the References section which follows the notes.

Analysis of Musical Characteristics

As indicated above, while music itself is of major concern for the sociologist of music, it is often a most difficult subject to discuss and analyze.[1] It should be recognized from the outset that some types of recording and playback devices are most instrumental in this kind of effort. While one may be able to distinguish various musical characteristics aurally, the general absence of an appropriate terminology to describe such experience makes a discussion difficult. What, for instance, are the qualities that render a particular composition "sad" or "cheerful," "exciting" or "boring"? While musical training would allow one to identify rhythm, tempo, key of the composition, chord progressions and melody line, other avenues of research must be followed for much that is sociologically significant.

A term used frequently in the popular music industry which may also have application for most serious music is the *hook*. A hook is a particular segment of the composition which is particularly attractive or noticeable to the listener, and often appears at the beginning of a composition, such as the "da da da dum" which begins Beethoven's Fifth Symphony. In other cases, a hook may be the use of a particular instrument (often the banjo in commercial sound tracks) or a distinctive rhythmic background. It would be possible to have subjects listen to selected recordings and ask them to identify any features of the recording that they find immediately noticeable, and to further describe their feelings about these features. If this concept of the "hook" is valid (and experience suggests it is), then there should be a high degree of agreement among respondents in the identification of its presence. Whether a particular hook elicits similar responses is a question which deserves further research. If the cooperation of a music group could be secured, an interesting test of the concept of the hook would be to produce several recordings of a given composition with different hooks and then obtain a measurement of the respondents' reactions to these changed characteristics. Another research question which has yet to be explored is that of the use of various hooks in music over a given historical period. Important questions would include the frequency of use of a particular type of hook, the variety of hooks used in a given period, the variation of hooks among different styles of music.

Another musical distinction which does not require much specialized musical expertise is that of the instrumentation used in the performance of a particular composition or in a general style. In bluegrass, for example, five or six instruments (banjo, fiddle, bass fiddle, acoustic guitar, mandolin, and Dobro guitar) are commonly used. Beyond the identification of instruments, it is also possible to identify the use of particular instruments for solo passages or for the accompaniment of solos and vocals. In bluegrass, again, it is common practice for the different instruments to each take a turn at a solo part between vocals, with the instruments also taking a noticeable accompanying role behind the vocal which precedes their solo passages. The observation of such phenomena provides the kind of first material from which analyses may be made.

When the compositions under study involve vocal performance, it is also possible to identify the arrangement of voices. Among many possibilities are: performance by a single performer; a single performer with a chorus background; joint performance by two or more performers; alternation of vocals by several performers; singing in unison or harmony; and variations in the pitch and intensity of the vocalists. Careful listening to a collection of recordings will allow the development of a classification system based on the above characteristics. This type of analysis would allow the examination of questions about the presence of solo versus group vocals in various types of popular musical styles over time. Does a particular musical style have a higher frequency of one type of vocal arrangement than another style? Are female vocal groups less prevalent in one time period than in another? There are other questions as well which could be addressed in this way. A classification system using characteristics such as these has been developed by Alan Lomas (1962) for the study of cross-cultural variations in folk music, but it has many applications yet to be realized in the study of commercial and serious music.

Content Analysis of Lyrics

Perhaps the most common analytic technique used by sociologists in the study of popular music is the analysis of lyrical content. The identification of themes in lyrics is usually accomplished by a small group of individuals who are asked independently to read the lyrics in question and to identify the "message" in the lyrics. When these judges agree on a theme, then the analyst has obtained the information necessary for a comparison of different compositions. This is evident in the analysis of themes of courtship and autonomy in popular songs, as found in the research of Horton (1957), Carey (1969), and others. It should be noted in passing that song lyrics are frequently available from music stores in the case of popular songs, but that the analyst may be forced to transcribe lyrics from recordings. An obvious reason for the popularity of content analysis is that it is straightforward and simple in its own way; lyrics may be treated as any other text. Questions concerning the significance of song lyrics have been raised by Hirsch (1969) and others, however, whose findings indicate that a majority of listeners are not able to identify the "message" of lyrics. Hirsch suggests that the lyrics may tell more about the values of the songwriter than those of the listener. Despite the uncertainty about the significance of song lyrics, they remain an area of research for additional development; of many possible questions, one which should prove interesting would be an examination of differing interpretations of lyrics by members of various social groupings. Would age, race, geographic location, sex, or other characteristics reveal signficant differences in the perceived meaning of a given set of lyrics? Just as the presence of a high degree of consensus over the meaning of a lyric would be significant, so would consensus within a particular grouping.

Music Production

This area of music research will be mentioned only briefly, since it generally relies on traditional means of data collection. If the situation in question is of such a nature that participation in music production is possible (e.g., the researcher is an accomplished musician who can take part), then certainly participant observation would provide a wealth of information. In other cases unobtrusive and nonreactive approaches might be more appropriate. Careful observation of verbal and non-verbal communication among musicians and between musicians and audience can reveal valuable information about these and other relationships (Webb et al., 1966). Supplemented by the more customary methods of survey research and interviewing, these techniques can provide important information relevant to a variety of areas.

Recording companies also provide information about music

production. Most recording studios retain information from recording sessions, information which indicates the musicians involved, instruments used, vocalists, songs recorded, and time and date of recording. Such recording data are particularly available for country music, through the Country Music Foundation in Nashville, Tennessee. The area of music production is extremely interesting and important for the sociology of music. Music-making is a social act with several dimensions: the composer and performer implicitly assume the role of another in their creative activities, and this other may include both a general audience as well as other musicians and composers (whether or not they are physically and temporally present). Previous studies of role-taking processes have numerous applications to this area (see Stebbins, 1976).

Music Distribution

There have been a number of significant studies of the music industry with specific emphasis on the promotion and distribution of records. The methods used generally have been traditional techniques and need little elaboration here.[2] A major question in the study of distribution concerns the way decisions are made about the products to be distributed. Such diverse individuals as record company executives, wholesale and retail record dealers, and radio disc jockeys seem to play roles in this process. It is clear that of the thousands of records produced each year, only a few become successful; a part of this success must inevitably be tied to decisions made by these individuals respecting the potential success of each recording. There have been some studies of the selection of compositions for performance by orchestras (Mueller, 1973), but much remains to be done. While it may be relatively easy to identify who selects particular recordings, the criteria which are used are far from obvious and have yet to be systematically studied. Data about music distribution are not readily available but may be obtained from some sources. The printed programs of orchestra and band performances can serve as an indication of selection patterns. In addition, radio stations maintain "playlists," which vary considerably in reliability. The music industry maintains information on sales, but the latter may be distorted by differences between wholesale and retail sales and the industry's various marketing techniques.

Consumption

Hand in hand with distribution is the equally important matter of who acquires music and what is done with it. Several studies of this topic have been made by means of interviews of persons leaving concerts and persons making purchases in record stores, as well as questionnaires which solicited similar information regarding type and frequency of music consumption. Less extensively examined is how music is used by individuals. There is some evidence (Dees and Vera, 1978) which suggests that there is a pattern to the method by which people choose music for specific purposes, with a relationship between particular musical characteristics and the activities involved.

Another indication of music consumption can be obtained from various music industry trade publications, such as *Cashbox* and *Billboard*. In addition to publishing regular listings of popular records, they also often carry information about the number of musical instruments, phonographs, and related items sold annually. Although the techniques used by *Cashbox* and *Billboard* for the determination of music popularity have varied over the past decade, they nevertheless represent the best sources of information on the subject.[3]

Another interesting area of music consumption is the use of music as a means of manipulating others. This is quite evident in the playing of patriotic songs by bands, but also present in a more subtle form in the phenomenon of background music, which may be found in so many commercial and business settings. The companies which provide this service to retail stores, restaurants, medical offices, and other locations offer a product which is intended to produce a desired behavior on the part of the listener (Mussulman, 1974).

Sources in Disciplines Other than Sociology

For the sociologist of music, professional journals in music are an obvious source of insight and information. Particularly important is work in ethnomusicology and the journal which bears that name. In addition, the fields of psychology and music therapy often produce studies and research reports which have a great potential for use by sociologists. Many of the psychological

studies are concerned with musical ability, perception, and training, and the music therapy field is particularly concerned with the
beneficial effects of making and listening to music. Finally, the
Journal of Psychophysics regularly publishes research which has
direct applications to musical phenomena.

It should be observed in conclusion that one of the reasons
that the sociology of music holds such an interest for people who
come to it either through the social scientific or musical approaches
is the potential for the development of new areas of inquiry. The
techniques discussed here and the studies suggested do not begin
to exhaust the questions left to be asked and answered; they
simply identify some of the more obvious directions for the interested person to go.

Notes

1. Music as a Mentality

1. The term *conduct* is preferred to *behavior* because conduct is activity guided by thinking. Understanding, self-knowledge, and other kinds of thinking will not directly influence behavior, such as heartbeats and eye blinks. Behavior is more properly the concern of animal psychology and biology rather than of sociology.

2. On the biographical aspect of the history of the arts, see J. H. Mueller, 1938: 223, and Dufrenne, 1967: 316. References are given to authors' names, date of publication, and page number; full bibliographic information appears at the end of the book.

3. Again there is the problem of private-but-social music. An experienced musician who plays her or his own composition in private is taking the role of at least three actors: composer, performer, listener. The form of the activity is social even if the census count does not exceed one.

4. These arrangements will be discussed in more detail in chapter 4.

5. M. Kaplan (1951: 347) notes that little attention has been paid to centers which are removed from the areas of mass consumption of music; with these alternative centers seems to come a relative freedom from box office considerations, newspaper critics, and impresarios.

6. A more detailed discussion can be found in Gurvitch, 1962.

7. Kaplan's distinction appears to have been derived from Gotshalk, 1947: 157-163. Wright (1975) uses a more specialized phraseology wherein musical meanings are "congeneric" while nonmusical meanings are "extrageneric."

8. We are setting aside altogether meanings which are purely personal or which are unique to the related biographies of a small number of people. For example, M. Kaplan (1951: 98) speaks of meanings derived in home life: "the achievements of the child as she progresses with her piano lessons become a psychological pattern of continuity to all the family, with a recognizable past, present, and plans for the future: it provides, through such experiences as periodic performance or recitals, little crises with their corresponding tensions and satisfactions."

9. The conductor, Jesus Lopez-Cobos, points to simplifications introduced into Donizetti's scores for the benefit of second-rate orchestras, as well

157

as to copying mistakes introduced by the Ricordi house and transpositions created for certain kinds of vocal soloists; see Reuling, 1978.

10. We are ignoring for the moment the issue of "tone deafness." Physical hearing problems are not at issue in sociology, except as interaction patterns develop around them — e.g., the deaf role, labeling, passing as a non-deaf person, etc.

11. See also J. H. Mueller, 1963: 216.

12. In addition, the very idea of freshness, etc., as opposed to what it is that is considered fresh, changes. Modern composers cannot emulate past works, adding their own personal touch, as did J. S. Bach, W. A. Mozart, Beethoven and Wagner at the beginning of their compositional careers. The classics are now so familiar that "derivative" qualities are easily detected and not accorded equal respect with the classics; see J. H. Mueller, 1951: 285.

13. This is in addition to the fact that identical score markings have different meanings in different eras and traditions. The meaning of "presto" is historically relative; the intriguing fact, however, is that the validity of published metronome markings is equally relative.

14. Earlier formulations of this analysis appeared in Blasi, Dasilva and Weigert, 1978: 323–336, and Blasi, 1977.

15. The *naturalisme* of Zola evidently stemmed from the dual influence of natural science, on the one hand, and a ground-breaking novel of Edmond and Jules de Goncourt, *Germinie Lacerteux* (1865), on the other. The latter was an account of the wretched life of a servant. The Italian novelist Verga realized that he could use the naturalist approach in short stories and plays about the poor of his native Sicily. Mascagni and Puccini were well acquainted with both Zola and Verga, and Mascagni's *Cavalleria Rusticana* is based on one of Verga's exposes of Sicilian life. The similarity between stage and life is a claim around which Leoncavallo's *I Pagliacci* is structured, thereby directly embodying the naturalist philosophy. See Kestner, 1978.

16. Verdi's *Otello* is a good example of music written with the scenic totality in mind from beginning to end. The musical meaning unfolds only in a dialectic with the dramatic situation and would be lost if the score were played in isolation from it.

17. See Adorno, 1965: 72, 78; and 1976: 80.

2. Participation in Music

1. Nash (1955) lists the following in the U.S.: League of Composers, International Society for Contemporary Music, Society for the Publication of American Music, American Composers' Alliance, Koussevitzky Foundation, National Association of American Conductors and Composers. The League of Composers, founded in 1923, published the journal *Modern Music* from 1924 to 1947; its influential members included Aaron Copeland and Virgil

Thompson, the focal persons in the "Francophile" school of modern American music. The International Society for Contemporary Music was founded in Europe in 1922 to organize concerts of the music of the Second Viennese School — Schoenberg, Berg and Webern. Its American section, bolstered by central European refugees from Nazism, comprised the "Germanophile" school of modern American music. Because the Americans felt discriminated against by the Europeans after World War II, they merged with the League in 1954, forming League-ISCM, which organizes concerts for contemporary American composers to this day; see Rockwell, 1980.

2. Not too surprisingly, they are likely to have developed a passion for music at an early age and to have come from musically active families; for some reason they are overwhelmingly male (Nash, 1957). The early family focus on music contrasts with the childhood environment of most popular songwriters (Etzkorn, 1959: 299).

3. Publishers usually return unsolicited songs unread as a protection against accusations of plagiarism. On the fate of song compositions in general, see Etzkorn, 1959: 18-26.

4. Some readers may be interested in the kinds of issues which come to be negotiated between the copyright holders associations and colleges and universities. Under current American law, fees are owed for noneducational uses, such as entertainment. For an account of the negotiation of the model contract for colleges and universities, see Magarrell, 1980a and 1980b.

5. There are also conflicts which originate in factors other than that which is endemic to music communication. Film producers may have an eye on potential sound track album sales and thus confuse pop hit songwriting with film scoring, or they may demand unrealistically aesthetic music for a hack-quality film. Even success is not an unqualified blessing for a film composer; doing well with a murder mystery, for instance, may result in an unwanted stereotype so that all that one is called upon to do is score murder mysteries — e.g., reapplying the same old themes in a television detective series (Faulkner, 1978: 108-113).

6. Schleiermacher calls this *nachkenstruiren* (1838: 17, 20, 32, 96, 215) and *Nachbilden* (1838: 39; and 1836: 207, 358) or *nacherfinden* (1838: 214). The notions of *nachbilden, erleben* and *nacherleben* were also used by Dilthey (1921-36: V: 263-264, VII: 224ff.) and Simmel (1892: 77). The similar notion of *inneres nacherschaften* is used by Unger (1929: 30). As internal reproduction the concept is found even in Droysen (1937: 328) and several other authors.

7. Dilthey, 1921-36: V: 265; VII: 120, where he speaks of a *zurück-übertragen*.

8. Humboldt, 1903-36: VII: 56ff.; Segond, 1930: 184; Carnelutti, 1942: 139-143.

9. Schleiermacher, 1838: 7: "Hermeneutic, while not theory but art of interpretation, is as much an art of understanding and does not involve the exposition of the understanding."

10. See a similar distinction by Jacob Grimm, quoted in Jolles, 1930: 226.

11. This distinction is discussed by Furtwängler, (1948: 9) and Parente (1936: 218ff.); see also Hartmann (1949: 421ff.).

12. Against such a historicist tendency see Furtwängler, 1949: 100ff. A similar technical approach, with a discretionary, subordinate character, occurs in dramatic interpretation, in particular when it is a matter of going beyond the indetermination left regarding some point in the role of a character; see Stanislavskii, 1936: 278ff. Moreover, even in this field, as well as that of law, discretion does not mean being arbitrary but trying to bring forth the best that is reflected in the scope of the pre-given work (von Herrnritt, 1921: 299ff.).

13. See P. Abraham (1960), "Interpretation," in the *Encyclopedie Française*.

14. Penetrated by a concrete duration, in the sense of Bergson's *durée*.

15. See Furtwängler, 1948: 62-64, 11, 28, 56ff., 71, 99-100; Nietzsche, 1924: I: 327; Rothacker, 1954: 259.

16. Faulkner, 1973b: 336 lists the respectable competitors as: Atlanta, Baltimore, Buffalo, Cincinnati, Dallas, Denver, Detroit, Houston, Indianapolis, Kansas City, Los Angeles, Milwaukee, Minneapolis, Montreal, New Jersey, New Orleans, Pittsburgh, Rochester, St. Louis, San Antonio, San Francisco, Seattle, Toronto, and Washington.

17. Westby (1960: 225) observed: "Hiring of string players for whatever outside jobs are to be had is effected through a long-time member of the orchestra who acts as a one-man employment agency. . . . He starts with the players at the front of the sections and works toward the back. . . ."

18. In phenomenological language, the conductor marks the polythetic experience desired.

19. The term *rehearsal* is not here used in the sense of the old European custom of having "rehearsals" for invited guests, celebrities and critics prior to performances which were open to the paying public.

20. A parallel situation occurs with opera vocalists, but in recent years, with the rise of the importance of the stage director in an area where the conductor was once supreme, the situation is more complex. "Singers often object to the overall concepts of the production—that is, the integration of the ideas of the conductor, director, and designer. The issues are usually posed at rehearsal, and the star performer participates in the conflict resolution" (Martorella, 1974: 290).

21. "The folklore of the studios is full of rich anecdotes about the abilities of performers to play anything at sight, in any style, to follow any conductor no matter what his abilities, and do this efficiently, with precise intonation, phrasing, and attack" (Faulkner, 1971: 7).

22. Sutherland's list of less prestigious companies included the Metropolitan Opera Ballet, the Manhattan Festival Ballet, the Boston Ballet, the Pennsylvania Ballet, the Chicago Opera Ballet, the San Francisco Ballet, the National Ballet, and the Atlanta Civic Ballet.

23. Adorno's translator uses the closest English word, *resentment*,

which does not quite duplicate the meaning. *Resentiment* refers to an attitude which arises from repressing envy, the attitude which leads one to be extra nice to a person who is extremely lucky. By chosing such uncomplimentary designations Adorno makes obvious his own preference for the expert listener.

24. "While works of art hardly ever attempt to imitate society and their creators need know nothing of it, the gestures of the works of art are objective answers to objective social configurations. They have often been designed to meet the needs of the consumer; more frequently, they stand in a contradiction to his need." (Adorno, 1973: 132)

25. An exception may be the case of tap dancing, where the foot taps are supposed to be integrally related to the music rhythm.

26. The following account closely follows Dees, 1978.

3. Social Organization and Music

1. While the data analysis by Kaplan and his assistants left something to be desired, the report is informative in its sweep of topics, and the "reading of the situation" is often insightful.

2. The Metropolitan Opera is a case of a company whose program is so large that it has outgrown the New York metropolitan area population base. Thus, it has had to build a constituency throughout the United States and Canada through radio and television broadcasts and a guild magazine. It receives cash gifts through such means, as well as political support for federal funds, the latter justified by the organization's serving as a stimulus for opera throughout the U.S. (Netzer, 1978: 117-125).

3. "Le problème de la misère materielle du peuple y est abordé pour inciter à des attitudes de résignation et de patience. La situation social de sous-développement y est expliquée par des causes surnaturelles" (Souffrant, 1970: 431).

4. Calculated from Conyers, 1963. Forty percent found satisfaction in singing to themselves, 32 percent in musical activities at school, 31 percent in singing in formal groups, 28 percent in listening to jukeboxes, 21 percent in playing instruments, 14 percent in playing instruments for others, 10 percent in singing for others, 5 percent in composing, 3 percent in writing lyrics.

5. In the days of national radio "hookups" the publishers hired "pluggers" to persuade bandleaders to play their music. The pluggers were a relentless crew who frequented nightspots and indiscriminately pushed everything on their list with high pressure techniques (see M. Kaplan, 1951: 63-64).

6. A parallel with the "charts" is found in medieval through Victorian England, where vagrant singers — often harassed by lawmen — found what people responded to, reported their observations to printers, and sold pages of lyrics or sheet music on their travels (Lloyd, 1967: 31-32).

7. Lloyd, 1967: 15-16. Lloyd notes that the great student of English

folk song, Cecil J. Sharp (see Sharp, 1907), was a socialist who romantically identified with the lower classes (Lloyd, 1967: 14).

8. See Peterson and diMaggio, 1975. It is noteworthy that Etzkorn (1959: 296) found that serious music composers were likely to come from professional- and business-class backgrounds while popular songwriters came from a wide spectrum of class backgrounds.

9. For a more extended discussion of kinds of rationality, see G. H. Mueller, 1979. Advancing a discussion begun by Max Weber, Mueller distinguishes among *purposive action* as rationality, *organizing actions and values* as rationality, and *formal and technical system* as rationality.

10. Riesman (1957) used the terms *majority* and *minority* in a statistical rather than an ethnic sense. His essay, based on interviews with adolescents, originally dates from 1951.

11. One of the authors witnessed an interesting expression of the social stance of soul music in a 1970 Mardi Gras parade in New Orleans. A black marching band ceased playing but continued marching to the firm, rhythmic chant, "Soul...soul...soul." The chant came from a squad of girls, who held their fists closed as they marched. This held the silent attention of the bystanders.

4. Illustrative Studies

1. The term *banjo* is here used to refer to the five-string instrument. While there have been a number of different types of banjos, the five-string model is the oldest and best known. Also worthy of study is the tenor banjo, a four-string instrument popular in early jazz and western swing in the early twentieth century.

2. For a more detailed account of the history of the banjo's development, see Bacon (1930), Bailey (1972), Bluestein (1954), Epstein (1975), Heaton (1970), and Seeger (1962).

3. Epstein's survey (1975) of historical accounts of early banjos is quite interesting in providing descriptions and explanations of various observers. Also, see Nettl's (1960: 56) discussion of the African bania.

4. Nathan, 1962. The influence of African music systems on the development of American music has been outlined elsewhere, particularly with respect to rhythmic patterns and the use of flatted fifths and sevenths; see Waterman, 1952.

5. Joel Sweeney, a Virginia minstrel, is usually credited with the invention of the fifth string (see Seeger, 1962; Scruggs, 1968), but Bailey (1972) challenges the accuracy of such stories.

6. By the end of the nineteenth century, simple but sturdy banjos were available for only three or four dollars from such firms as Sears and Roebuck.

7. There are a great many terms which are often used interchangeably with frailing, although current purists would argue that each term represents

a distinct variation. Among the more common terms are *clawhammer, down-picking, rapping,* and *beating.*

8. The drone function served by the fifth string is fairly unique in Western music, but often found in other cultures; see Reck, 1977: 276-284.

9. For a list of various tunings for the banjo, see Sandberg and Weissman, 1976. The modal tunings were derived from the ballad and fiddle tune traditions of the British Isles and were retained in the isolated areas of the Appalachians, particularly the use of five-tone (pentatonic) scales (Reck, 1977: 218).

10. The introduction of the banjo to the mountains is unclear, since slaves were primarily found in the lower flat areas where plantations existed. Some researchers suggest that traveling minstrels introduced it, while Bluestein (1954) argues that it was brought in by slaves building railroads.

11. For the clash of religion and dancing in the mountains, see Campbell, 1972: 130-131.

12. Although the classical style of banjo playing almost disappeared in this century, the recent interest in the banjo and bluegrass music has prompted some musicians to revive the technique. By 1978, several recordings and instruction books for classical banjo were generally available to the public.

13. One example of those performers in the classical style is Charles Dobson, who, with his mother, gave concert performances in the U.S. and England, introduced several modifications to the banjo, and published one of the earliest instruction manuals.

14. Some of the musicians who used two- or three-finger styles who are known by musicologists today are Dock Boggs and Snuffy Jenkins. For additional discussion of the finger-picking tradition in North Carolina, see Heaton, 1970.

15. Because so many of the string bands were composed of family members, they are often referred to as "brother groups." It was very common for one brother to play guitar and another mandolin, with others (if any) adding other instruments. During this time, the guitar and mandolin became probably the most common and popular country instruments. For additional discussion, see Malone, 1968: 126-129.

16. Among the earliest recordings by a country music performer which clearly reveal the influence of "blues" notes are the songs of Jimmy Rodgers; see Malone, 1968: 83. For a discussion of the influence of other musical forms on country music, see Malone, 1968: 21-23.

17. Malone, 1968: 239-270, discusses the development of the "Nashville sound" and the general massification of the country music audience. These developments were the culmination of processes which began immediately after World War II.

18. The vocal style of harmony was closely associated with the shaped note and Sacred Harp singing of the southern churches, especially in the use of parallel thirds and the high harmony part sung above the melody. In bluegrass singing today, this influence still remains, with the harmony parts iden-

tified as tenor, baritone, and bass, indicating not a particular range of the voice but rather the distance of the harmony part from the melody.

20. The typical pattern would be for each solo instrument (fiddle, mandolin, banjo) to take a passage between each verse and chorus; the other instruments would accompany, interjecting louder notes as decorative elements at the end of passages and under sustained notes of the solo. While this sort of improvisation is not the same as that found in contemporary jazz, it does bear a similarity to earlier jazz forms and reveals the common influence of the call and response pattern of early blues.

21. One probably inaccurate legend holds that the term *bluegrass* referred to Monroe himself and was used in requests made of Flatt and Scruggs for the former employer's, Monroe's, numbers. See Artis, 1975: 47.

22. For a more detailed discussion of the melodic style, see Trischka, 1976, where interviews with several musicians who early adopted the style are presented.

23. Flatt and Scruggs' record company seized on the commercial potential of bluegrass as "folk music." A number of their albums were produced in the 1960s with the intention of attracting the folk and folk-rock audience. These contained songs by such composers as Woody Guthrie and Bob Dylan (Artis, 1975: 51-52). Flatt and Scruggs were among the first bluegrass groups to play in "respectable" places such as Jordan Hall in Boston (December 18, 1961) and Carnegie Hall in New York (December 8, 1962). Many of the banjoists who developed melodic style were college-educated; some had formal music training. A variation of the melodic style, chromatic style, is similar in technique but has arpeggios including a series of consecutive notes rather than just those of the melody (Trischka, 1976).

24. Examples are the Osborne Brothers and Jim and Jesse and the Virginia Boys.

25. The introduction of drums and electric guitars to the stage of the Grand Ole Opry occurred in gradual steps; see Shelton and Goldblatt, 1966: 125.

26. In addition to the promotion of Flatt and Scruggs' albums as folk music, there was the music for the motion picture "Bonnie and Clyde" and the television program "Beverly Hillbillies." Commercial advertising and radio and television frequently use bluegrass music and especially the banjo as background.

27. The notion of "false consciousness" is used here following the classical discussion of Karl Marx and F. Engels (in *German Ideology* and *Theses on Feuerbach*). The difference between false and liberated consciousness is not that between error and truth but is a functional difference related to the purpose served by thought in the collective life of mankind. "Wrong" thinking is that which confirms the state of human servitude and is unaware of its own proper function; emancipated thought is the affirmation of humanity, enabling man to develop his native abilities. See also Leszek Kolakowski, *Main Currents of Marxism*, vol. 1 (New York: Oxford University Press, 1981), 175.

28. Phrase used by the NAACP referring to the educated elite of the black community.

29. This may have been paralleled in more recent times. Comparing responses of middle-class blacks living in integrated areas with those of middle-class blacks living in traditionally black neighborhoods, Bullough (1967) found that the latter felt less able to control events influencing their lives. The possible implication is that the community itself affected the respondents in the segregated areas in such a way that they were more fatalistic.

30. Black college students in the South may have reacted to their own talent in a way similar to Joplin, when they responded to a survey which showed that academic self-confidence was closely related to nontraditional achievement aspirations (Gurin, 1970: 625).

31. Consider Stravinsky, *Histoire du Soldat*, and Villa-Lobos' use of Portuguese terms for moods, etc.

32. *Second Quartet with Voice.*

33. Stravinsky, "Berceuse du Chat"; Villa-Lobos, "Three Indian Poems."

34. Villa-Lobos, in a series of works for piano and voice, such as *Xangô, Estrela e Lua Nova, Ganide Iune, Nozani-Na,* etc.

35. Stravinsky, *Pribaoutki*; Villa-Lobos, *Epigramas.*

36. Schönberg; Stravinsky's *Octeto*; Villa-Lobos in certain of the *Choros,* and *Noneto, Rude Poem, Trio for Wind Instruments, Amazon.*

37. Interview, *O Globo*, Rio de Janeiro, December 19, 1942.

38. The first examples of suites are found in lute music of the sixteenth century.

39. Later other types of dances were added or served as replacements. Among them are the minuet, gavotte, branle, bourrée, passepied, and the passacaille.

40. A brief description of the character of the dances may illuminate the situation. The allemande, a lively and very low keyboard dance of German origin, was still popular at the beginning of the nineteenth century. The tune was in two beats, the movement of a little animated allegretto. Before the spread of the Italian titles, composers would often use the label "allemande" to indicate the tempo of allegretto in their work. The courante, a dance borne out of the alleys and avenues of Paris, is like a slow sarabande. The sarabande is a noble dance of a severe character. It is similar to a slow and somber minuet. The gigue, of German (*Gige, Geige,* violin) or Scotch origin, is a lively dance typically found in the French ballets of the sixteenth century. Its movement is rapid, light, quite gay.

41. Debussy used the suite form in *Pour le Piano, Suite Bergamasque, Etampes,* and *Images.*

42. In Bach's case, the work was definitely of a pedagogical character, intended as an instrument for technical training. Nonetheless, the composer's genius raised it much above the level of an exercise text. In Robert Schumann's case, the character of the work is different. Writing to Clara Schumann, he says, "You will like them, but you must forget that you are a virtuoso." The

pieces were to be considered "reminiscences" from childhood; thus, their writing was purified and their technical demands minimal. They represented a quite mature work as befitting the position of the creator. Adorno comments on other similar cases of the childish quality in music: "Debussy's child-likeness was a game of the man who knows himself and his own limits; Stravinsky's is an oblique attack on the grown-up world; Ravel's alone was the aristocratic sublimation of sorrow" (Adorno, 1964: 70). Thus, for Adorno, the same characterological attribute of music can be interpreted in different ways, depending upon its position in a composer's work. In Debussy's case, the childlike character of the music expresses the cynicism or bourgeois self-consciousness; in Stravinsky, the powerlessly rebellious perspective of youth; and in Ravel's "aristocratic music" it is the combination of play and grief, an interaction of opposites, which Adorno implies, came closest of the three representations to an awareness of truth.

43. A similar design is used by Villa-Lobos in the piano piece *Lenda do Caboclo* (Rio, 1929). It is a two-part piece, the first part in a moderato muito dolente, which is followed in order by a transitional sequence in piu mosso, a very expressive andantino, a transitional sequence poco allegre, and ending with a double repetition of the first tempo.

44. Also present for instance, in Jorge Amado's *Gabriela, Clove,* and *Cinnamon* (1972).

45. Much came by way of Afro-Brazilian cults, particularly in ritual songs. These are replete with both melodic materials and rhythm; one can recall, for instance, the *pontos de santo* in candombles of Bahia, or even in the *macumbas* of Rio de Janeiro.

46. Note for instance contrasting compositions in *Caracará* by Joao do Vale and José Candido, and in *Chegança* by Edu Lobo and Oduvaldo Viana Filho, which is included in the recording *Brazil: Sertao and Favelas* (Paris: Le Nouveau Chansonnier, La Chanson Rebelle, no. 1, Le Chant du Monde).

Appendix: Research Methods in the Sociology of Music

1. For a review of the sociology-musicology relationship, see Etzkorn, 1974.

2. For an example of analysis of the music industry, see Peterson and Berger, 1975.

3. Gillespie and Perry (1973) present a good discussion of non-reactive strategies in the study of acceptance of artistic products.

References

Abraham P.
1960 "Interpretation." *Enclyclopedie française*, vol. 17. Paris: Societé de gestion de l'Enclyclopedie française.

Adorno, Theodor W.
1955 *Kulturkritik und Gesellschaft*. Frankfurt. Suhrkamp.
1963 *Dissonanzen; Musik in der verwalteten Welt*. Göttingen: Vendenhoeck und Ruprecht.
1964 *Moments Musicaux: Neugedruckte Aufsätze, 1928 bis 1962*. Frankfurt: Suhrkamp, 1964.
1971 "Sociologie de la musique." *Musique en jeu* (1971): 7-15.
1973 (1948) *Philosophy of Modern Music*. Translated by Anne G. Mitchell and Wesley V. Bloomster. London: Sheed and Ward.
1976 (1962) *Introduction to the Sociology of Music*. Translated by E. B. Ashton. New York: Seabury.

Adorno, Theodor W., and George Simpson
1941 "On popular music." *Studies in Philosophy and Social Science* 9: 17-48.

Andrade, Mario de
1936 *Ensaio sobre a Musica Brasileira*. Sao Paulo: L. G. Miranda.
1938 *Musica, doce musica*. Sao Paulo: L. G. Miranda.
1940 *Modinhas Imperials*. Sao Paulo: L. G. Miranda.

Artis, Bob
1975 *Bluegrass*. New York: Hawthorne Books.

Bacon, Fred J.
1930 "The evolution of the banjo." *Music Trades* 87: 26.

Bailey, Jay
1972 "Historical origin and stylistic development of the five string banjo." *Journal of American Folklore* 73: 58-65.

Becker, Howard S.
1951 "The professional dance musician and his audience." *American Journal of Sociology* 57: 137-144.
1953 "Some contingencies of the professional dance musician's career." *Human Organization* 12: 22-26.
1963 "Careers in deviant occupational group: the dance musician." In Becker, *Outsiders, Studies in the Sociology of Deviance*, pp. 101-119. New York: Free Press.

167

Bennett, H. Smith
1979 "Secondary popular culture." *Symbolic Interaction* 2:1: 117–125.
Bensman, Joseph
1967 "Classical music and the status game." *Transaction* 4:9 (Sept.): 54–59.
Bensman, Joseph, and Israel Gerver
1958 "Art and the mass society." *Social Problems* 6:1: 4–10.
Bensman, Joseph, and Robert Lilienfeld
1970 "A phenomenological model of the attitudes of the performing artist." *Journal of Aesthetic Education* 4:2: 107–119.
Berger, Morroe
1947 "Jazz: resistance to the diffusion of a culture pattern." *Journal of Negro History* 32: 461–494.
Berger, Peter L., and Thomas Luckmann
1967 *The Social Construction of Reality: A Treatise in the Sociology of Knowledge.* Garden City, N.Y.: Doubleday.
Bettencourt, Gastao de
1945 *Historia Breve da Musica no Brasil.* Lisbon: SNI–Coleçao Atlântico.
Blasi, Anthony J.
1977 "Phenomenology and the sociology of grand opera." Paper presented at the meeting of the Midwest Sociological Association in Minneapolis.
Blasi, Anthony J., Fabio B. Dasilva, and Andrew J. Weigert
1978 *Toward an Interpretive Sociology.* Washington: University Press of America.
Blaukopf, Kurt
1974 "New patterns of musical behaviour of the young generation in industrial societies." In Irmgard Bontinck, ed., *New Patterns of Musical Behavior of the Young Generation in Industrial Societies,* communications presented to the international symposium, Vienna 1972, organized by the International Institute for Music, Dance and Theatre in the Audio-visual Media, pp. 13–30. Vienna: Universal Edition AG.
Bluestein, Gene
1954 "America's folk instrument: notes on the five string banjo." *Western Folklore* 23: 241–251.
Blumer, Herbert
1969 "Fashion: from class differentiation to collective selection." *Sociological Quarterly* 10: 275–291.
Bogg, Richard A., and Daniel Fair
1974 "Hallucinogenic drugs and rock music." *Indiana Academy of the Social Sciences Proceedings,* Third Series, 9: 146–155.
Bullough, Bonnie
1967 "Alienation in the ghetto." *American Journal of Sociology* 72: 469–478.
Burman, Patrick, Fabio B. Dasilva, et al.
1975 "Freud and Marx: structural homologies in interpretive schemes." *Indiana Academy of the Social Sciences Proceedings* 10: 164–171.

Cameron, William Bruce
1954 "Sociological notes on the jam session." *Social Forces* 33: 177-182.
Campbell, John C.
1921 *The Southern Highlander and His Homeland.* New York: Russell Sage.
Candido, Antonio
1964 *Os Parceiros do Rio Bonito.* Rio de Janeiro: José Olímpio Editora.
1973 "Literatura e cultura de 1900 a 1945." *Literatura e Sociedade.* Sao
      Paulo: CEN.
Canton, Dario
1968 "El mundo de los tangos de Gardel." *Revista Latino-americana de
      Sociologia* 4:3: 341-362.
Carey, James T.
1969 "The ideology of autonomy in popular lyrics: a content analysis."
      Psychiatry 32:2: 150-164.
Carnelutti, Francesco
1942 *Meditazioni,* vol. 1. Rome, Milan: Tumminelli.
Conyers, James E.
1963 "An exploratory story of musical tastes and interests of college stu-
      dents." *Sociological Inquiry* 33:1: 58-66.
Cottle, Thomas J.
1966 "Social class and social dancing." *Sociological Quarterly* 7:2: 179-196.
Couch, Stephen R.
1976 "Class, politics, and symphony orchestras." *Society* 14:1: 24-29.
Damrell, Joseph
1977 *Seeking Spiritual Meaning. The World of Vedanta.* Beverly Hills: Sage.
Dasilva, Fabio B.
1979 "Misleading discourse and the message of silence: an Adornian intro-
      duction to Villa-Lobos' music." *International Review of the Aesthetics
      and Sociology of Music* 10:2: 167-180.
Dasilva, Fabio B., and David R. Dees
1975 "The social realms of music." Paper presented at the meeting of the
      American Sociological Association in San Francisco. (Later version:
      "The social context of music." *Revue Internationale de Sociologie,*
      special issue, summer 1976.)
Dasilva, Fabio B., and Jim Faught
1982 "Nostalgia: perspectives on an American ideology from the Frank-
      furtian critical school." *Qualitative Sociology* 5:1 47-62.
Davies, Evan
1969 "Psychological characteristics of Beatle mania." *Journal of the History
      of Ideas* 30:2: 273-280.
Dees, David R.
1972 "On the Theory of Art: A Structuralist Analysis with Example from
      Contemporary Popular Music." Ph.D. diss., University of Notre Dame.
1978 "Social control processes in informal music groups." Paper presented

at the meeting of the Mid-South Sociological Association in Jackson, Mississippi.

Dees, David R., and Hernan Vera Godoy
1978   "Soundtracking everyday life: the use of music in redefining situations." *Sociological Inquiry* 48:2: 133–141.

Denisoff, R. Serge
1966   "Songs of persuasion: a sociological analysis of urban propaganda songs." *Journal of American Folklore* 79: 581–589.
1969   "Folk music and the American left: a generational-ideological comparison." *British Journal of Sociology* 20:4: 427–442.
1970   "The religious roots of the American song of persuasion." *Western Folklore* 29: 175–184.
1971   *Great Day Coming: Folk Music and the American Left.* Urbana: University of Illinois Press.

Denisoff, R. Serge, and Mark H. Levine
1971   "The popular protest song: the case of 'Eve of Destruction.'" *Public Opinion Quarterly* 35:1: 117–122.
1972   "Youth and popular music: a test of the taste culture hypothesis." *Youth and Society* 4:2: 237–255.

Dilthey, Wilhelm
1921-36 *Gesammelte Schriften.* Leipzig and Berlin: G. B. Teubner.

Droysen, J. G.
1973   *Historik; Vorlesungen über Enzyklopädie und Methodologie der Geschichte.* Munich and Berlin: Oldenbourg.

DuBois, W. E. B.
1967   (1899) *The Philadelphia Negro: A Social Study.* New York: Schocken.

Dufrenne, Mikel
1967   *Phenomenologie de l'experience esthetique.* Vol. 1: *L'Objet esthetique.* Paris: Presses Universitares de France.

Epstein, Dena J.
1975   "The folk banjo: a documentary history." *Ethnomusicology* 19: 347–371.

Etzkorn, K. Peter
1959   "Musical and Social Patterns of Songwriters: An Exploratory Sociological Study." Ph.D. diss., Princeton University.
1974   "On music, social structure and sociology." *International Review of the Aesthetics and Sociology of Music* 5:1: 43–49.
1976   "Manufacturing music: Music differentiation complements social differentiation." *Society* 14:1 19–23.

Fathi, Asghar, and Carole L. Heath
1974   "Group influence, mass media and musical taste among Canadian students." *Journalism Quarterly* 51:4: 705–709.

Faulkner, Robert
1971   *Hollywood Studio Musicians: Their Work and Careers in the Recording Industry.* Chicago: Aldine-Atherton.

1973a "Orchestra interaction: some features of communication and authority in an artistic organization." *Sociological Quarterly* 14: 147-157.

1973b "Career concerns and mobility motivations of orchestra musicians." *Sociological Quarterly* 14: 334-349.

1974 "Making us sound bad: performer compliance and interaction in the symphony orchestra." In Phyllis L. Stewart and Muriel G. Cantor, eds., *Varieties of Work Experience: The Social Control of Occupational Groups and Roles*, pp. 238-248. Cambridge, Mass.: Schenckman.

1978 "Swimming with sharks: occupational mandate and the film composer in Hollywood." *Qualitative Sociology* 1:2: 99-129.

Federico, Ronald C.

1974 "Recruitment, training, and performance: the case of ballet." In Phyllis L. Stewart and Muriel G. Cantor, eds., *Varieties of Work Experience: The Social Control of Occupational Groups and Roles*, pp. 249-260. Cambridge, Mass.: Schenckman.

Fernandes, Florestan

1973 *Capitalismo Dependente e Classes Sociais na America Latina.* Rio de Janeiro: Sahar Editora.

Fischer, J. L., and Marc J. Swartz

1960 "Socio-psychological aspects of some Trukese and Ponapean love songs." *Journal of American Folklore* 73: 218-224.

Fox, William S., and James D. Williams

1974 "Political orientation and music preferences among college students." *Public Opinion Quarterly* 38:3: 352-371.

Furtwängler, Wilhelm

1948 *Gespräche über Musik.* Vienna: Humboldt Verlag.

Gadamer, Hans-Georg

1975 *Truth and Method.* New York: Seabury.

Gammond, Peter

1975 *Scott Joplin and the Ragtime Era.* London: Angus and Robertson.

Gillespie, David F., and Ronald W. Perry

1973 "Research strategies for studying the acceptance of artistic creativity." *Sociology and Social Research* 58: 48-55.

Goldmann, Lucien

1964 *The Hidden God: A Study of Tragic Vision in the Pensées of Pascal and the Tragedies of Racine.* Translated by Philip Thody. London: Routledge and Kegan Paul.

1969 *The Human Sciences and Philosophy.* Translated by Hayden V. White and Robert Anchor. London: Cape.

Gotschalk, D. W.

1947 *Art and the Social Order.* Chicago: University of Chicago Press.

Gramsci, Antonio

1975 *The Modern Prince and Other Writings.* New York: International.

Greisman, H. C.

1976 "Disenchantment of the world: romanticism, aesthetics and sociological theory." *British Journal of Sociology* 27: 495-507.

Gurin, Patricia
1970   "Motivation and aspirations of southern negro college youth." *American Journal of Sociology* 75: 607–631.
Gurvitch, Georges
1962   *Dialectique et sociologie.* Paris: Flammarion.
1972   *The Social Frameworks of Knowledge.* Translated by Margaret A. Thompson and Kenneth A. Thompson. New York: Harper Torchbooks.
Hanslick, Eduart
1881   *Vom Musikalisch-Schönen.* Leipzig: Barth.
Haralambos, Michael
1970   "Soul music and blues: their meaning and relevance in northern United States black ghettos." In Norman E. Whitten, Jr., and John F. Szwed, eds., *Afro-American Anthropology: Contemporary Perspectives,* pp. 367–383. New York: Free Press.
Hartmann, N.
1949   *Das Problem des geistigen Seins; Untersuchungen zur Grundlegung der Geschichtsphilosophie und der Geisteswissenschaften.* Berlin: de Gruyter.
Harvey, Edward
1967   "Social change and the jazz musician." *Social Forces* 46:1: 34–41.
Heaton, Cherrill P.
1970   "The five string banjo in North Carolina." *Southern Folklore Quarterly* 35: 82–97.
Herrmann von Herrnritt, Rudolf
1921   *Grundlehren des Verwaltungsrecht.* Tubingen: Mohr.
Hesbacker, Peter, Robert Downing, and David G. Berger
1975   "Sound recording popularity charts: a useful tool for music research." *Popular Music and Society* 4: 3–18.
Hirsch, Paul
1969   *The Structure of the Popular Music Industry: The Filtering Process by Which Records Are Pre-selected for Public Consumption.* Ann Arbor: Institute for Social Research, University of Michigan.
Hofstadter, Richard
1955   *Social Darwinism in American Thought,* revised edition. Boston: Beacon.
Horkheimer, Max, and Theodor W. Adorno
1972   *Dialectic of Enlightenment.* Translated by John Cumming. New York: Seabury.
Horton, Donald T.
1957   "The dialogue of courtship in popular songs." *American Journal of Sociology* 62:6: 564–578.
Humboldt, Wilhelm
1903–36 *Gesammelte Schriften.* Berlin: Behr.

Husserl, Edmund
1962   *Ideas: General Introduction to Pure Phenomenology*. London: Collier-Macmillan.
1970   *The Crisis of European Sciences and Transcendental Phenomenology: An Introduction to Phenomenological Philosophy*. Evanston, Ill.: Northwestern University Press.
Jarvie, I. C.
1972   *Concepts and Society*. London: Routledge and Kegan Paul.
Jefferson, Thomas
1955   *Notes on the State of Virginia*. Chapel Hill: University of North Carolina Press.
Jolles, Andre
1930   *Einfache Formen*. Halle: Niemeyer.
Jones, Robert
1975   "'Treemonisha': Scott Joplin's ragtime opera struts its stuff on Broadway." *Opera News* 40:3 (Sept.): 12-15.
Jules-Rosette, Bennetta
1975   "Song and spirit: the use of song in the management of ritual settings." *Africa* 45:2: 150-166.
Kadushin, Charles
1969   "The professional self-concept of music students." *American Journal of Sociology* 75:3: 389-404.
Kaplan, Arlene A.
1955   "A study of folksinging in a mass society." *Sociologus* 5:1: 14-28.
Kaplan, Max
1944   "Music in the City: A Sociological Survey of Musical Facilities and Activities in Pueblo, Colorado." Mimeograph.
1951   "The Musician in America: A Study of His Social Roles. Introduction to a Sociology of Music." Ph.D. diss., University of Illinois.
1955   "Telopractice: a symphony orchestra as it prepares for a concert." *Social Forces* 33: 352-359.
Kasdan, Leonard, and Jon H. Appleton
1970   "Tradition and change: the case of music." *Comparative Studies in Society and History* 12:1: 50-58.
Kestner, Joseph
1978   "Out of the tinder box." *Opera News* 42:20 (April 8): 11-14.
Kohler, Wolfgang
1947   *Gestalt Psychology*. New York: Liveright.
Lastrucci, Carlo L.
1941   "The professional dance musician." *Journal of Musicology* 3:3: 168-172.
Lehman, L.
1935   *Droit de l'artiste*. Paris: Vrin.
Levine, Mark H., and R. Serge Denisoff
1972   "Demographic variable and record ownership by collegiates: a research note." *Popular Music and Society* 1:2: 94-107.
Lloyd, A. L.
1967   *Folk Song in England*. New York: International.

Loft, Abram
1950 "Musicians' Guild and Union: A Consideration of the Evolution of Protective Organization among Musicians." Ph.D. diss., Columbia University.

Lomax, Allan
1962 "Song structure and social structure." *Ethnology* 1: 425–451.

Lovell, Terry
1973 "Weber, Goldman and the sociology of beliefs." *Archives européennes de sociologie* 1:2: 304–323.

Lukàcs, Georg
1971 *History and Class Consciousness: Studies in Marxist Dialectics.* Translated by Rodney Livingston. Cambridge, Mass.: Massachusetts Institute of Technology Press.

Lund, Jens, and R. Serge Denisoff
1971 "The folk music revival and the counter culture: contributions and contradictions." *Journal of American Folklore* 84: 394–405.

Maduro, Otto
1976 *Marxismo y Religion.* Caracas: Monte Avila Editores.

Magarrell, Jack
1980a "Colleges to pay higher music-copyright fees." *Chronicle of Higher Education,* Feb. 19, p. 5.
1980b "New license for copyrighted music will reduce red tape but raise prices." *Chronicle of Higher Education.* Mar. 31, p. 4.

Malhotra, Valerie Ann
1979 "Weber's concept of rationalization and the electronic revolution in western classical music." *Qualitative Sociology* 1:3: 100–120.

Malone, Bill C.
1968 *Country Music USA.* Austin: University of Texas Press.

Mannheim, Karl
1971 *From Karl Mannheim,* edited by Kurt H. Wolff. New York: Oxford University Press.

Marcuse, Herbert
1972 "Art and revolution." *Partisan Review* 39:2: 174–187.

Martorella, Rosanne
1974 "The Performing Artist as a Member of an Organization: A Sociological Study of Opera Performers and the Economics of Opera Production." Ph.D. diss., New School for Social Research.
1977 "The relationship between box office and repertoire: a case study of opera." *Sociological Quarterly* 18:3: 354–366.

Marx, Karl
1967 "Toward the critique of Hegel's philosophy of law: introduction." In *Writings of the Young Marx on Philosophy and Society,* translated and edited by Lloyd D. Easton and Kurt H. Guddat, pp. 249–264. Garden City, N.Y.: Anchor Doubleday.

Mashkin, Karen D., and Thomas J. Volgy
1975 "Socio-political attitudes and musical preferences." *Social Science Quarterly* 56:3: 450–459.
Merriam, Alan P., and Raymond W. Mack
1960 "The jazz community." *Social Forces* 38:3: 211–222.
Middleton, Richard
1972 "Cage and the meta-Freudians." *British Journal of Aesthetics* 12: 228–243.
Mueller, G. H.
1979 "The notion of rationality in the work of Max Weber." *Archives européennes de sociologie* 20:1: 149–171.
Mueller, John H.
1935 "Is art the product of its age?" *Social Forces* 13:367–375.
1938 "The folkway of art: an analysis of the social theories of art." *American Journal of Sociology* 44: 222–238.
1951 *The American Symphony Orchestra.* Bloomington: Indiana University Press.
1963 "A sociological approach to musical behavior." *Ethnomusicology* 7:3: 216–220.
Murdock, Graham, and Robin McCron
1973 "Scoobies, skins and contemporary pop." *New Society* 29 (March): 690–692.
Mussulman, Joseph A.
1974 *The Uses of Music.* Englewood Cliffs, N.J.: Prentice-Hall.
Nash, Dennison
1955 "Challenge and response in the American composer's career." *Journal of Aesthetics and Art Criticism* 14: 116–122.
1957 "The socialization of an artist: the American composer." *Social Forces* 35: 307–313.
1964 "The alienated composer." In Robert N. Wilson, ed., *The Arts in Society*, pp. 35–60. Englewood Cliffs, N.J.: Prentice-Hall.
Nathan, Hans
1962 *Dan Emmett and the Rise of Early Negro Minstrelsy.* Norman: University of Oklahoma Press.
National Council of the Arts
1973 *Arts and the People.* New York: Cranford Wood.
Nettl, Bruno
1960 *An Introduction to Folk Music in the United States.* Detroit: Wayne State University Press.
Netzer, Dick
1978 *The Subsidized Muse: Public Support for the Arts in the United States.* New York: Cambridge University Press.
Nietzsche, Friedrich Wilhelm
1924 *Human, All Too Human*, vol. 1. New York: Macmillan.

Odum, Howard W., and Guy B. Johnson
1964 (1925) *The Negro and His Songs: A Study of Typical Negro Songs in the South.* Hatboro, Pa.: Folklore Associates, Inc. Originally published by University of North Carolina Press.
Ortega y Gasset, José
1975 "An essay in esthetics." In *Phenomenology and Art,* translated by Philip W. Silver, pp. 127–150. New York: Norton.
Parente, Alfredo
1936 *La musica e le arti; problemi di estetica.* Bari: Laterza.
Pearsall, Ronald
1975 *Edwardian Popular Music.* Rutherford, N.J.: Farleigh Dickinson University Press.
Peterson, Richard A., and David G. Berger
1971 "Entrepreneurship in organizations: evidence from the popular music industry." *Administrative Science Quarterly* 16:1: 97–107.
1975 "Cycles in symbol production: the case of popular music." *American Sociological Review* 40:2: 158–173.
Peterson, Richard A., and Russell B. Davis, Jr.
1974 "The contemporary American radio audience." *Popular Music and Society* 3:4: 299–313.
Peterson, Richard A., and Paul di Maggio
1975 "From region to class: the changing country music: a test of the massification hypothesis." *Social Forces* 53:3: 497–506.
Portelli, Hugues
1972 *Gramsci et le bloc historique.* Paris: Presses Universitaires de France.
Price, Steven D.
1975 *Old as the Hills.* New York: Viking Press.
Ramos Tinhorao, José
1974 *Pequena Historia da Musica Popular, da Modinha à Cançao de Protesto.* Petrópolis: Editora Vozes Ltda.
Reck, David
1977 *Music of the Whole Earth.* New York: Charles Scribner's Sons.
Reuling, Karl F.
1978 "Autograph seeker: Jesus Lopez-Cobos prefers to conduct from the original." *Opera News* 42:17 (March 11): 22–23.
Ricoeur, Paul
1973 "Ethnics and culture." *Philosophy Today* 17: 153–165.
Rieger, Jon H.
1974 "The coming crisis in the youth music market." *Popular Music and Society* 4: 19–35.
1978 "Tradition and change in symbol systems: sociological observations on the reconstruction of concepts of music." Paper presented at the meeting of the North Central Sociological Association in Cincinnati.

Rieger, Jon H., and Brian Rublein
1974   "Whiteman as the Don Quixote of jazz." *Popular Music and Society*
         3:1: 3-23.
Riesman, David
1957   "Listening to popular music." In Bernard Rosenberg and David
         Manning White, eds., *Mass Culture: The Popular Arts in America*, pp.
         408-417. Glencoe, Ill.: Free Press.
Rinzler, Ralph
1976   "Roots of the folk revival." In Larry Sandberg and Dick Weissmann,
         eds., *The Folk Music Sourcebook*, pp. 114-117. New York: Knopf.
Robinson, Harlow
1980   "Going to the opera — Moscow style." *New York Times* (April 13),
         section 2: 1-25.
Rockwell, John
1980   "Signs of vitality in new music." *New York Times*, Feb. 10.
Rooney, James
1971   *Bossmen: Bill Monroe and Muddy Waters*. New York: Dial Press.
Rose, Gillian
1978   *The Melancholy Science: An Introduction to the Thought of Theodor
         W. Adorno*. New York: Columbia University Press.
Rosenbaum, Art
1968   *Old-Time Mountain Banjo*. New York: Oak Publications.
Rosenberg, Neil V.
1967   "From sound to style: the emergence of bluegrass." *Journal of Ameri-
         can Folklore* 80: 215-218.
1974   *Bill Monroe and His Blue Grass Boys: An Illustrated Discography*.
         Nashville: Country Music Foundation Press.
Rosenblum, Barbara
1978   "Style as social process." *American Sociological Review* 43: 422-438.
Rothacker, Erich
1954   *Die dogmatische Denkform in den Geisteswissenschaften und das
         Problem des Historismus*. Wiesbaden.
Ryser, Carol Bierson
1964   "The student dancer." In Robert W. Wilson, ed., *The Arts in Society*,
         pp. 97-121. Englewood Cliffs, N.J.: Prentice-Hall.
Sandberg, Larry, and Dick Weissman
1976   *The Folk Music Sourcebook*. New York: Knopf.
Schleiermacher, Friedrich Ernest Daniel
1836   *Friedrich Schleiermachers sämtliche Werke*, Bd. 3. "Reden und
         Abhandlungun." Berlin: Reimer.
1838   *Hermeneutik und Kritik mit besonderer beziehung auf das Neue Testa-
         ment*. Berlin.

178   References

Schuessler, Karl
1948   "Social background and musical taste." *American Sociological Review* 13: 330–335.
Schutz, Alfred
1951   "Making music together: a study in social relationship." *Social Research* 18:1: 76–97. Reprinted pp. 159–178 in Alfred Schutz, Collected Papers II, *Studies in Social Theory*, edited by Arvid Brodersen. The Hague: Martinus Nijhoff, 1976.
1956   "Mozart and the philosophers." *Social Research* 23:2: 219–242. Reprinted pp. 179–200 in Alfred Schutz, Collected Papers II, *Studies in Social Theory*, edited by Arvid Brodersen. The Hague: Martinus Nijhoff, 1976.
1972   *The Phenomenology of the Social World.* Translated by George Walsh and Frederick Lehnert. London: Heinemann.
1973   "Symbol, reality and society." Pp. 287–356 in Alfred Schutz, Collected Papers I, *The Problem of Social Reality*, edited by Maurice Natanson. The Hague: Martinus Nijhoff.
Schwartz, Roberto
1967   "Nota sobre a vanquarda e o conformismo." *Teoria e Practica* (Sao Paulo): 2.
1970   "Remarques sur la culture et la politique au Bresil." *Les Temps Modernes*: 33–73.
Scruggs, Earl
1968   *Earl Scruggs and the Five String Banjo.* New York: Peer International.
Seeger, Pete
1962   *How to Play the Five String Banjo.* Beacon, N.Y.: published by the author.
Segond, Joseph Louis Paul
1930   *Traité de psychologie.* Paris: Colin.
Sharp, Cecil J.
1907   *English Folk-song, Some Conclusions.* London.
Shelton, Robert, and Burt Goldblatt
1966   *The Country Music Story.* Secaucus, N.J.: Castle Books.
Silbermann, Alphons
1963   *The Sociology of Music.* Translated by Corbet Stewart. London: Routledge and Kegan Paul.
Simmel, Georg
1892   *Probleme der Geschichtsphilosophie.* Leipzig: Dunker and Humboldt.
1904   "The sociology of conflict." *American Journal of Sociology* 9:4: 490–525.
Slotkin, J. S.
1943   "Jazz and its forerunners as an example of acculturation." *American Sociological Review* 8: 570–575.
Sontag, Susan
1978   "Illness as metaphor." *The New York Review of Books*, Jan. 26:10–16.

Sorokin, Pitirim A.
1969   *Society, Culture, and Personality: Their Structure and Dynamics.* New York: Cooper Square.

Souffrant, Claude
1970   "Un Catholicisme de resignation en Haiti. Sociologie d'un recueil de cantiques religieux." *Social Compass* 17:3: 425-438.

Stanislavski, Konstantin S.
1936   *An Actor Prepares.* New York: Theatre Arts.

Stebbins, Robert A.
1965   "A historical and experimental design for the study of a jazz community." *Indian Sociological Bulletin* 2:4: 228-242.
1966   "Class, status, and power among jazz and commercial musicians." *Sociological Quarterly* 7:2: 197-213.
1969   "Role distance, role-distance behaviour, and jazz musicians." *British Journal of Sociology* 20:4: 406-415.
1976   "Music among friends: the social networks of amateur musicians." *Revue Internationale de Sociologie* 12:1: 52-73.

Stone, Gregory A.
1965   "Appearance and the Self." In Mary Ellen Roach and Joanne Bubolz Eicher, eds., *Dress, Adornment and the Social Order.* New York: Wiley.

Sudnow, David
1978   *Ways of the Hand: The Organization of Improvised Conduct.* Cambridge, Mass.: Harvard University Press.

Supicic, Ivo
1964   "Problemes de la sociologie musicale." *Cahiers Internationaux de Sociologie* 37: 119-129.

Sutherland, David Earl
1976   "Ballet as a career." *Society* 14:1: 40-45.

Szwed, John F.
1966   "Musical style and racial conflict." *Phylon* 27:4: 358-366.

Taubman, Howard
1951   *The Maestro: The Life of Arturo Toscanini.* New York: Simon and Schuster.

Toffler, Alvin
1967   "The art of measuring the arts." *Annals of the American Academy of Political and Social Science* 373: 141-155.

Trischka, Tony
1976   *Melodic Banjo.* New York: Oak Publications.

Unger, Rudolf
1929   *Aufsatze zur Prinzipienlehre der Literaturgeschichte.* Berlin: Junker und Dunnhaupt.

Valkman, Otto
1974   "Some methodological aspects of preferences in pop music." In Irmgard Bontinck, ed., *New Patterns of Musical Behavior of the Young Generation in Industrial Societies,* pp. 33-43. Communications Pre-

sented to the International Symposium, Vienna, 1972, organized by the International Institute for Music, Dance and Theatre in the Audio-visual Media. Vienna: Universal Edition A.G.

Vassberg, David E.
1969   "Villa-Lobos: music as a tool of nationalism." *Luzo Brazilian Review* (1969): 55–65.

Waterman, Richard A.
1952   "African influences on the music of the Americas." In Sol Tax, ed., *Acculturation in the Americas*, pp. 207–218. Chicago: University of Chicago Press.

Webb, Eugene, Donald T. Campbell, Richard D. Schwartz, and Lee Sechrest
1966   *Unobtrusive Measures: Nonreactive Research in the Social Sciences.* Chicago: Rand McNally.

Weber, Max
1946   "Religious rejections of the world and their directions." In *From Max Weber: Essays in Sociology*, translated and edited by H. H. Gerth and C. W. Mills, pp. 323–359. New York: Oxford University Press.
1958   (1921) *The Rational and Social Foundations of Music*, translated by Don Martindale, Johannes Riedel, and Gertrude Neuwirth. Carbondale, Ill.: Southern Illinois University Press.

Weitzman, Ronald
1971   "An introduction to Adorno's music and social criticism" *Music and Letters* (1971): 287–298.

Wenk, Arthur
1976   *Claude Debussy and the Poets.* Berkeley: University of California Press.

Wenz, Joseph
1929   *Kinderlied und Kindersseéle.* Kassel: Barenreiter Verlag.

Wernick, Peter
1974   *Bluegrass Banjo.* New York: Oak Publications.

Westby, David L.
1960   "The career experience of the symphony musician." *Social Forces* 38:3: 223–230.

Wright, Derrick F.
1975   "Musical meaning and its social determinants." *Sociology* 9:3: 419–435.

Index

181